Descriptosaurus:
Action & Adventure

Descriptosaurus: Action & Adventure builds on the vocabulary and descriptive phrases introduced in the original bestselling *Descriptosaurus* and, within the context of adventure stories, develops the structure and use of the words and phrases to promote colourful cinematic writing. This essential guide will enable children to take their writing to the next level, combine their descriptions of setting and character and show how the two interact. Children can then experiment with their own adventure stories, armed with the skills, techniques and vocabulary necessary to describe their action scenes in a way that allows the reader to feel the characters' fear and excitement, and visualise the action within the setting.

This new system also provides a contextualised alternative to grammar textbooks and will assist children in acquiring, understanding and applying the grammar they will need to improve their writing, both creative and technical.

Alison Wilcox has extensive teaching experience in schools in England and Scotland. Colleagues describe her methods as 'innovative and inspirational to even the most reluctant of writers'.

Descriptosaurus

Action & Adventure

Alison Wilcox

Routledge
Taylor & Francis Group

LONDON AND NEW YORK

First published 2016
by Routledge
2 Park Square, Milton Park, Abingdon, Oxon OX14 4RN

and by Routledge
711 Third Avenue, New York, NY 10017

Routledge is an imprint of the Taylor & Francis Group, an informa business

British Library Cataloguing in Publication Data
A catalogue record for this book is available from the British Library

Library of Congress Cataloging-in-Publication Data
Wilcox, Alison
    Descriptosaurus: genres: action and adventure/Alison Wilcox
        pages cm
    1. Creative writing (Elementary education) 2. Literary form—
    Study and teaching (Elementary) 3. Adventure stories. I. Title.
    LB1576.W48757 2015
    372.62'3—dc23   2015007987

ISBN: 978-1-138-85868-8 (hbk)
ISBN: 978-1-138-85869-5 (pbk)
ISBN: 978-1-315-71777-7 (ebk)

Typeset in Myriad Pro
by Keystroke, Station Road, Codsall, Wolverhampton

MIX
Paper from
responsible sources
FSC FSC® C013056
www.fsc.org

Printed and bound in Great Britain by
TJ International Ltd, Padstow, Cornwall

Contents

Introduction

BACKGROUND

When I first decided to write *Descriptosaurus* it was because my experience of teaching creative writing to children had revealed that many had great imaginations and lots of ideas, but did not have the descriptive vocabulary to communicate these effectively. This was partly due to a lack of reading or a passive involvement with a text so that the techniques and vocabulary were not absorbed. I have been delighted with the response to the original work and have seen many fabulous examples of descriptive writing.

After writing *Descriptosaurus,* I returned to the classroom to conduct further research on different ways to use the resource. It became evident that one of the weaknesses in children's texts was the way they connected their writing. Often the pace of their writing was dramatically slowed by lengthy, unnecessary detail because they didn't have the vocabulary to move the story on to another scene. I also found that displaying the text on the whiteboard and modelling the process was extremely effective. This was why the second edition included a CD and a section on connectives and adverbs.

NATIONAL LITERACY TRUST – DESCRIPTIVE WRITING COMPETITION

In 2013, I collaborated with the National Literacy Trust on a descriptive writing competition. I was astounded by the response and the quality of the entries. I think that too much attention is given to the apparent decreasing standards in schools, particularly in literacy, and not enough media attention given to the outstanding young writers and teachers in our classrooms today. The work and support of the National Literacy Trust are vital in maintaining and improving these standards.

WHY WRITE *DESCRIPTOSAURUS: ACTION & ADVENTURE?*

As part of the process, the National Literacy Trust analysed the genres children chose in their descriptive pieces. It is important that children are given the opportunity to develop their interests and passions. To ensure that children are engaged and enthused with creative writing, it is vital that they are, where possible, given a choice. The four genres that stood out as by far the most popular were: ghost stories; adventure; fantasy; and myths & legends, which is why we have decided to concentrate on these four areas.

When brainstorming ideas for an adventure story, the discussion is enthusiastic and the ideas literally 'pour out'. However, children find it difficult to express their ideas in a coherent, written form. They can visualise the scenes, but don't have the vocabulary and techniques to transfer them to paper. Action scenes, in particular, often prove disappointing, with the action ending up with a brief act of violence. My research has shown that boys often focus on action scenes across all genres, so it is important that they are given the tools to commit their visions to paper, and provided with alternatives that build up suspense, rather than that one violent act.

S/C-I-R: SETTING/CHARACTER, INTERACTION, REACTION

It was also evident that the action scenes were just a list of various actions, with no description of the setting, other characters or emotions. On other occasions, I have seen excellent descriptions of settings, but the characters do not move (interact) through the setting. They are disjointed pieces of description. I have, therefore, been experimenting with a new system I have called 'S/C-I-R' (Setting/Character-Interaction-Reaction), which has resulted in cinematic writing of an exceptional standard.

The resulting work has described the setting, moved the character through the setting, and described their reactions to what they see or the events in which they are involved. A model of the S/C-I-R structure is included at the beginning of each chapter.

CONTEXTUALISED GRAMMAR LEARNING

Another benefit of this system has been to provide a contextualised alternative to the prescriptive, repetitive focus on textbook grammar in response to the introduction of the SPAG tests. Taking a number of sentences or phrases for setting, interaction and reaction, combining them into a descriptive paragraph of an action scene, and then experimenting with different ways of combining the sentences, openers and length is a very engaging way of learning about grammar and its impact on the flow, sense and expression. I have also noticed that the discussion that results from this experimentation has a dramatic impact on the quality of responses to comprehension tasks.

The exercise can be extended to changing tenses, including adverbs, or even using it to write a scene for a playscript. These exercises can be done as extended sessions, as part of the planning, or as warm-up exercises. They are also excellent for modelled and collaborative learning.

Different focuses can be used. For example:

- ★ Giving the class three sentences all starting with pronouns, and setting them the challenge of using different ways to open their sentences.
- ★ Asking them to use the three sentences to produce a paragraph of five or more sentences.
- ★ Blending the sentences, but changing them into the first person and present tense.

PLANNING AND EDITING

The age-old problem of ineffective planning and cursory editing still remains. To aid in this process, I have included a section in the Appendix on the structure and planning of an adventure story, breaking it down into manageable parts. A plot planning sheet is also included in the Appendix. Developing a habit of using a planning sheet to brainstorm ideas will, as we all know, greatly enhance the final piece of text. Hopefully, the structure of the planning sheet will also aid in the structure of the story.

To help with the development of strong characterisation, I have also included planning sheets for a hero and a villain.

To combat cursory editing, planning sheets are provided for action scenes, whether it be for 'the Race', 'the Chase' or 'Survival'. If phrases and sentences are collected for Setting/Character, Interaction and Reaction for each of the action scenes, and if the process of blending, altering and reducing that is practised in warm-up activities is used, hopefully the editing will become more focused and effective.

NON-FICTION

Adventure stories can be the focus for a lengthy unit, which can include many and varied non-fiction tasks. For example:

★ Safety manual for surviving an avalanche;
★ Fire drill instructions;
★ Discursive piece on the importance of being able to swim;
★ Diary entries about surviving in the desert, which can be extended to include hot-seating, a taped interview of the survivors, etc.
★ Travel brochure for a trip to an exotic location;
★ Advert for a competition for a place on an adventure expedition;
★ Recorded news item of the kidnap of a well-known personality;
★ Newspaper article on the capture of a dangerous villain.

I have had so much fun writing this book. It has been hard to stay focused on the brief, as I constantly found myself writing lengthy action scenes, which expanded into short stories. I hope all those who use *Action & Adventure* enjoy using it as much as I enjoyed writing it.

Alison Wilcox

Key elements

Adventure has been a common theme since the earliest days of written fiction. In fact, the origins of the adventure genre can be traced back to Homer's *Odyssey*, with its quests, dangerous journeys and heroism.

Adventure stories written specifically for children began in the nineteenth century, including, *Swiss Family Robinson*, *Children of the New Forest*, *The Adventures of Tom Sawyer* and *The Adventures of Huckleberry Finn*.

The expansion of the British Empire made adventure stories about journeys of discovery popular. Some famous writers at this time include Sir Walter Scott (*Rob Roy*), Robert Louis Stevenson (*Treasure Island*) and H. Rider Haggard (*King Solomon's Mines*).

Arthur Ransom developed the adventure story further by setting his stories in Britain rather than distant countries, while Rosemary Sutcliffe made the historical adventure novel popular, and Roald Dahl introduced an element of humour into his adventure stories.

Enid Blyton wrote many books from the 1940s onwards, and captured the main plot elements of children's adventure stories. Her books are still popular today with younger readers, as they include children:

- ★ with an exciting and often dangerous task to perform, such as finding hidden or lost treasure, or a prisoner in a locked tower;
- ★ pitted against villains, such as kidnappers and smugglers;
- ★ with many obstacles to overcome, including searching or being trapped in secret tunnels, caves, and underground passages, moors and mountains, islands, castles and old mansions.

Adventure has remained a very popular genre of fiction and has seen many changes over the years from:

- ★ stories of knights in armour to high-tech espionage;
- ★ swashbuckling pirate stories to time travel.

Adventure stories often overlap other genres, including:

- ★ Historical fiction (Rick Riordan)
- ★ Fantasy (J.R.R. Tolkien)
- ★ Spy stories (Anthony Horowitz).

FORM OF ENTERTAINMENT

The success of the adventure story lies in its ability to entertain and excite the reader – to carry them away from their daily routines at school and at home on an exciting and dangerous journey, transported on a tidal wave of action.

Adventure stories are packed with action, suspense, risk and excitement as the hero embarks on a journey filled with dangerous obstacles or has a villain to overcome, both of which make the hero's survival uncertain – with disastrous consequences should they fail.

The action scenes in stories for older children often involve fights but the emphasis is on suspense, escape and victory, rather than terror, gore and death.

A great adventure story is a gripping page-turner, which hooks the reader with its pace and thrills.

The tales often include:

- ★ A hero for whom the reader can root
- ★ An exciting undertaking involving physical danger (Quest)
- ★ A journey – dangerous, exotic locations
- ★ Obstacles to overcome
- ★ Life-or-death stakes, should the hero fail
- ★ A villain to fight against
- ★ Many twists and turns
- ★ Fast pace, drama
- ★ Excitement and suspense

- ★ Action sequences – struggles, fights, pursuit, chase, capture
- ★ Last-minute escapes
- ★ Cliffhangers.

A. THE HERO/HEROINE

An adventure story needs a hero that the reader wants to follow, and with whom they can empathise. (*For ease, I have referred to the hero (he), rather than alternating between 'hero' and 'heroine'.*) He should essentially be:

- ★ good and brave, but with no superhuman powers.

For the reader to be able to root for the hero, he has to be:

- ★ loyal and trustworthy, as this is what separates him from the villain.

That does not mean to say that the hero has to be perfect.

- ★ A hero with a flaw or an unusual or unexpected characteristic can make the story more interesting.
- ★ An unlikely hero is always an interesting twist. For example:
  - ☆ a character who is normally not very outgoing or known for their bravery but is an avid reader could be very useful in solving a problem, as he could have a wealth of information readily available. An excellent example of this is Hermione Granger in *Harry Potter*.
  - ☆ a technology whizz-kid not normally known for spending too much time outdoors.
  - ☆ a shy character who, as a result of previous bullying, has secretly been taking lessons in martial arts.

The London Eye Mystery by Siobhan Dowd is an excellent example of an unlikely hero. The hero, Ted, who appears to be autistic, solves the mystery as a result of his 'brain which works in its own unique way'.

It is also important that the hero develops or changes in some way as a result of his experiences.

Get to know your hero

- ★ Think of interesting or unusual people.
- ★ Collect ideas of heroes from books you have read.
- ★ Decide on a name.
- ★ How old is he?
- ★ Think of details that could be used in your physical description, such as their face, eyes, voice, hairstyle, clothes that reflect their personality, or skills.
- ★ Add a description of any distinctive features.
- ★ Who are his family and close friends?
- ★ What are his main interests?
- ★ Does he have a special talent?
- ★ What is he most afraid of? (This could be really important to the story, as you may want to make your hero face their worst fear as one of the obstacles they have to overcome.)
- ★ Does the hero or any of his family or friends have any secrets?
- ★ What has he got to gain by achieving the task, overcoming the challenge, or to lose by failing to do so?

Descriptions of heroes are not included in this book as detailed vocabulary and ideas are already included in the general *Descriptosaurus*, and the intention here is to offer advice and descriptive vocabulary specific to adventure stories.

B. THE VILLAIN

The hero needs an enemy to fight. The villain (referred to here as 'he') is usually:

- ★ disloyal, selfish, greedy, power-crazy.

It is possible that the villain and hero share the same goal – for example, recovering a valuable artefact. It is their *reason* for recovering it that is different.

Get to know your villain

- ★ Think of interesting or unusual people.
- ★ Collect ideas of villains from books you have read.

★ Decide on a name.
★ To present a villain as sinister or dangerous, he is often described using eyes, voice, expressions, movements and dark clothing.
★ Add a description of any distinctive features. For example, scars can be used as a hint to the reader that this character has had a violent past and therefore presents a dangerous and menacing threat to the hero.
★ Where does he live? What type of place is it? Is it very secure, scary? Is it in an isolated location?
★ What does the villain do for a living? Who are his allies?
★ Does he have a special talent?
★ Does he have any secrets?
★ What has he got to lose by the hero achieving the task?
★ What does he do to people who cross him?

C. QUEST, CHALLENGE

The hero has a problem to solve. This could be:

(a) **A challenge** – surviving in a storm, sandstorm, avalanche, earthquake, fire or a shipwreck;
(b) **A journey** – across a dangerous setting, for example, Antarctica, rainforest, mountains;
(c) **A quest** – usually to do with someone or something in danger and involving:

★ Rescue: an object or person, e.g. a valuable artefact, a kidnapped person;
★ Recovery: a modern invention, secret government documents, a medical breakthrough that could be abused for criminal purposes;
★ Discovery: a treasure map, a dangerous organisation;
★ Prevention: a disaster, conflict.

Make sure there is a good reason for making the journey or being in the setting. The consequences of failure must be so severe that the reader is aware that there is no going back and that the hero will have to face the many obstacles and dangers along the way until he reaches the end.

D. A DANGEROUS JOURNEY

The hero battles for survival:

- ★ against the elements, such as a storm on land, sea, desert, monsoon rains, floods, fire and explosions;
- ★ trapped in water, tackling rapids, lost in caves and tunnels;
- ★ whilst trapped in a natural disaster – earthquake, avalanche.

E. A SINISTER, DANGEROUS SETTING

- ★ In faraway, exotic locations, such as desert islands, rainforests; *or*
- ★ In a wood, cave, city, town, house, building, castle, graveyard near the hero's home.

The setting in an adventure story is where the:

- ★ adventure takes place;
- ★ the object or person being sought will be found;
- ★ unfinished business is resolved.

There may be a number of settings as the hero travels to his final destination, overcoming obstacles and evading the villain. Adventure stories often include a race or chase, where the hero hides, is followed, pursued, trapped, captured and escapes – which may all occur in different settings.

Key points

1. Decide why the setting is important to the story

If you are going to include chases and conflicts, think about how the setting will help stage these scenes.

(a) What features are there that the hero can:

- ★ leap on, across, climb up;
- ★ swing from;

* duck under, crawl under;
* hide behind.

(b) If the hero is trying to gain entry to the villain's location, or escape from the villain, is it the type of setting that could include **a secret passage**?

(c) What **barriers** are there to entering or escaping from the premises, location?

(d) What **obstacles** are there to retrieving the object or person that has been hidden/stored?

2. Think of words and phrases to help you build up the description of the setting

(a) Imagine you have a camera and move it around the location, then zoom in to pick up extra details.

(b) Map the location in a rectangle or series of shapes and plot the route of the race, chase, escape, making a note of important obstacles or items that will assist or prevent detection or capture.

3. Be descriptive

Use figurative language such as **similes** and **metaphors**. Some chapters have ideas for similes and metaphors included in the word section.

4. Use senses to bring the setting to life for your reader

As well as sight, think about what your character can:

* hear, smell, touch or taste.

5. To increase the tension, turn off the lights

This will mean that the hero has to rely on his other senses and makes it easier to include sounds, touch and smells, which adds to the tension.

F. ATMOSPHERE

It is the atmosphere that is created that increases the tension and makes the setting scary and the action scenes exciting – background noises, flickering lights and shadows, and tricky terrain, such as muddy or uneven ground during a chase.

(a) The key to writing a gripping adventure story is to withhold some information. At the beginning, the villain should be a background threat, a menacing shadow and presence. The initial threat should come from the villain's allies.

(b) Weather and darkness can be used to great effect to create a scary atmosphere and tension:

★ Howling winds
★ Mist or fog
★ Ferocious storms
★ Relentless rain
★ Dusk, shadows
★ Pitch black night.

For example:

> It was taking too long. The shadows spread and lengthened. She looked at her watch again. She should have heard something by now. All day she had been haunted by the feeling that she was being followed, and her fear grew as night fell. Fear of the unknown. Fear of what lurked in the shadows.

Add detail and description to paint a picture in the reader's mind. Giving a setting an atmosphere is more than just stating that 'It was quiet'. For example, adding more descriptive detail could give you:

> It was quiet. Too quiet! The birds had fallen silent and even the wind seemed to have died down. All was as still as death and dark as the grave.

G. SUSPENSE

Chapter 1, *Hooks*, includes a number of ideas and sentences on how to create suspense and give a hint to the reader about the danger to come, or that the danger is getting closer.

(a) **Entering the danger zone** – what's lurking behind the fence, gates, doors, trees, etc.?

(b) **Feeling of being followed/watched;**

(c) **Fear of discovery in a hiding place**, as footsteps/voices get closer; a snap of twigs nearby;

(d) **The villain or his allies gaining on the hero during the chase;**

(e) **Use of punctuation to add suspense:**

   ★ Include one or more sentences that hold back essential information from the reader until their ending.
   ★ Use colons, commas and repeated full stops to delay the revelation. For example:

   Opening the door to his room, he stopped dead in his tracks.

   She heard the squeak of footsteps, the creak of a door handle. Silence. A key turned in the door. The door creaked open . . . slowly opened wider. She dropped to her knees. Silhouetted in the doorway was . . .

(f) **Build a sense of urgency and panic by:**

   (i) Making frequent references to time (the 'ticking clock' effect):

   ★ He checked his watch again.
   ★ It was ten minutes to midnight. He had to get out by midnight.
   ★ Could he make it in time?
   ★ He searched desperately for a way out. Frantic now . . . time was running out.
   ★ He checked his watch again; his heart sank as he saw that there was now only one minute to go – and he was still trapped inside and no closer to finding a way out.

   (ii) Varying the length of the words, sentences and paragraphs, which increases the pace and the tension:

   ★ Use short words, e.g. *At once*, rather than, *Immediately*.
   ★ Place several short sentences consecutively, e.g. *She ducked. He lunged.*
   ★ Include one or two-word sentences, e.g. *Oh no!* or *Coming closer. Too close.*

★ When the action is the fastest, use partial sentences, e.g. *He had to get to the side. Had to reach the raft. He splashed, thrashed, kicked. Five strokes more. He lunged.*
★ Use short paragraphs – some may be a single line.
★ Include lots of verbs to convey action and create a fast pace. Use several verbs in a sentence.

H. OBSTACLES

Examples of obstacles the hero might have to face are:

★ ground (muddy, icy, uneven)
★ security surrounding the location (barbed wire fences, electric fences, alarms, security cameras, armed guards, savage dogs)
★ impenetrable forests, swamps
★ wild or poisonous animals
★ sheer mountains, flooded caves, labyrinth of tunnels
★ menacing villain and his allies
★ injuries sustained on the journey or inflicted by the villain.

I. EMOTION

Show how the hero reacts (emotion) to events, setting, villain, challenges, etc. The basic rule is the same as any other genre – 'Show not tell'.

(A) Reaction

Describing how a character reacts to events in the setting brings the scene to life for the reader and enables them to empathise with the character's situation and to root for the hero. For example:

He was terrified as he heard a warning yell . . . he had been spotted.

This *tells* the reader that the character is terrified, but does not show how the character *reacts* to the situation. Instead describe:

★ how he is feeling inside using, for example, heart or pulse
★ facial expressions

★ eyes
★ voice.

The same situation could be expanded to describe the character's reaction to the warning yell. For example:

An explosion of adrenalin surged through his body as he heard a warning yell . . . he had been spotted. Panic flooded his face as he saw several scuttling figures emerging out of the shadows. Scrambling to his feet, he began to move. As he glanced back, he was blasted by an explosion of terror. They were coming at him from all directions, and closing in on him with every step.

Note: The hero will experience many emotions during his adventure, but for the purposes of this book, the reactions for each section have been restricted to the particular emotions that you would expect the hero to have in those situations. For example:

★ The race – nervous
★ The chase – fear, despair
★ Survival – pain/exhaustion.

(B) Interaction: race, chase, conflict, capture

To add a cinematic quality to your writing, it is essential that the action scenes include a description of the character's movements – as they react to the events, to the villain and his allies, and move through the setting. The character may:

★ be frozen to the spot
★ move nervously, cautiously
★ duck behind a tree
★ move quickly – jump, spin, leap, whirl, dash, sprint
★ frantically look for a way of escape
★ move forward to defend himself.

Apart from enabling the reader to visualise their movements, the character's interaction is a signpost to the reader of the degree of danger and the closeness of the threat. For example:

She crouched on the ground. She was terrified of raising her head.

She darted and dodged around the furniture. Blundering and slipping on the wooden floor, she pushed her way past tables and chairs, sending lamps and ornaments clattering to the ground.

Part 1
The race

1

Hooks to build interest and tension

Note: Apart from aiding the flow of your writing, this chapter can also be used to stimulate quick, brainstorming activities to get your creative juices flowing by asking the questions – Why? How? When? Where? Who? What happened next? It is amazing how many stories can be created as a result of these quick activities.

OPENINGS

* They realised that somehow their old life had ended and a new one was about to begin.
* He would remember this moment later. When everything was normal and everyone in the room was still unaware of the approaching danger.
* Although he had no idea what it meant, he could sense that it was dangerous, that it was a warning. Warning him to get away while he still could.
* He could sense the danger prickling down his spine, the impending disaster. He was overwhelmed by the strange feeling that he alone could prevent it.
* It was days later that he would remember that moment.
* He listened carefully to the voice on the other end of the phone, but he had no idea how important this information was soon to become.
* They were nervous days while he waited for the knock on the door, for the phone to ring, but they didn't come. Not then.
* He knew he had to make the most difficult decision of his life.
* She lay awake night after night, heart filled with dread, recalling every detail of that dangerous offer.
* *Nowhere was safe anymore.*

* She had fallen asleep. For that, she would never forgive herself.
* How different things would have been if they had turned back.
* He knew he would never forget what he saw through that window. It turned out to be the worst decision he had made in a very long time.
* He should have followed them, or run the other way, but he stood frozen in shock as he turned the corner. And that was when everything started to go wrong.
* She knew she wouldn't be able to sleep, not after what she'd seen when his computer monitor flashed red.

WARNING OF DANGER TO COME

* Something deep inside, a sixth sense, warned her not to feel too secure.
* He couldn't shake off a sense of unease, a vague feeling that something was wrong, that he shouldn't have come.
* When they got there, a shock awaited them.
* He had a feeling he was delivering himself into a trap, but nothing could have prepared him for what he met around the next corner.
* Out of nowhere, the hairs on his neck rose.
* For a while things went well.
* A horrible suspicion started building inside her.
* He sensed something dark moving in the shadows, waiting for him. He knew the net was closing in, the noose tightening around his neck. Something bad was about to happen and there was no way of escaping it.
* He had a sinking feeling in his stomach about what lay ahead. He still couldn't be sure that he was doing the right thing. In the next hour, everything could go horribly wrong.
* It was a crazy idea. Every nerve in her body screamed at her to run . . . outside . . . away from the place. But making for an exit was not an option.
* It was only just the beginning of a new chapter of dangers. All day she had been haunted by the feeling that she was being followed. She sensed that a vast organisation was focusing all its energies on hunting her down.
* She tried to make sense of what she had heard. And as the truth dawned on her, she began to shake.
* He began to feel cold. Icy dread prickled his neck, warning him that danger was near.
* Ever since they had entered the place, she'd been fighting an underlying sense of panic.
* She put the key in the door, but something wasn't right; she sensed it before she opened the door.
* *All was still as death and dark as the grave.*
* It was very quiet. Too quiet!
* The night had been silent and now even the dawn chorus was still.

* Even the grandfather clock seemed to fall silent.
* The room fell silent. She could hear the ticking of the hall clock through the wall.
* When the breeze stopped, everything went very still and the wood became unnaturally quiet.
* Then there was silence. Even the wind seemed to have died down.
* It suddenly seemed frighteningly quiet. The air was charged with tension.
* Suddenly, the birds fell silent. Then one gave a high-pitched warning call.
* There were all sorts of rustlings and twitchings. They were probably nothing, just small creatures scampering into the undergrowth. But they reminded him that he had no right to be there.
* *An owl hooted and swept by on silent white wings.*
* A church bell began to chime in the distance.
* A scream from above caused his pulse to race. It was nothing more than a crow in the branches of a tree behind him.
* The wind howled. Great swirling gusts, relentless like an army of screaming banshees.
* *Shadows spread and lengthened. Their fear grew as night fell. Fear of the unknown. Fear of what lurked in the dark.*
* Twilight was closing in and she felt very uneasy.
* The last glowing embers of the fire slid into darkness.
* The shadows were now merging into one another, and the ground was being cloaked in the first shade of grey, heralding the night to come.
* It was dark with only flitting glimpses of the moon to keep them company.
* *The light was dwindling as the battery ran down.*
* His light flickered and went out. The battery was dead.
* Just then, the lights flickered off and for a second she was plunged into darkness.
* As she spoke, all the remaining lights went out. But for the occasional flash of lightning, everything was plunged into darkness.
* She stood in darkness so complete that when she held her hand in front of her nose, she couldn't even see its outline.
* In the windy, moonless dark, the house seemed dead, as if it had been left to rot and was now no more than a shuttered tomb.
* *The mist came in with the tide, smothering everything like a giant fleece.*
* They wandered like ghosts through the mist, guided by the murmuring of the river.
* The night wind swept over them, whispering through the trees, fashioning the mists into ghostly shapes that flung flickering shadows on the inky surface of the water.
* Behind him was pitch black, ahead sparsely scattered street lights.

THE TICKING CLOCK

- ★ His plan would buy him a few hours and nothing more.
- ★ When he opened his eyes, he guessed that a few hours must have passed. It was enough. It was time to make his move.
- ★ *A grandfather clock had been beating time as she hid in the shadows.*
- ★ He counted the time by the pace of the shadows creeping slowly across the ground.
- ★ *The hours dragged past.*
- ★ The minutes seemed to crawl.
- ★ The seconds ticked away, agonisingly slowly. It seemed to be taking for ever.
- ★ An hour passed, and then another and after a while . . .
- ★ In the long, agonising moments that followed . . .
- ★ *He saw that it was just after midnight.*
- ★ The grandfather clock boomed loudly, twelve times – midnight already.
- ★ Just as the town clock struck midnight . . .
- ★ She glanced nervously at her watch. And saw that it was just after midnight. They were late.
- ★ On every hour and half hour the church clock chimed.
- ★ *The next few minutes were going to be vital.*
- ★ Time was of the essence.
- ★ He glanced at his watch. Timing was essential. Twice he checked his watch. He glanced at his watch for a third time in ten minutes.
- ★ He had less than a second to make a decision.
- ★ It was too late to turn back now.
- ★ There was no time to worry. No time to think. He had to act now. Time had run out.
- ★ She knew she didn't have long to act. It had to be soon.
- ★ *The clock was ticking down.*
- ★ She couldn't afford to wait any longer.
- ★ 'If it's not too late', she thought.
- ★ He could feel the seconds ticking away.
- ★ He knew they were running out of time. They might be too late.
- ★ If he had arrived too late, everything he had been through had been for nothing.
- ★ She should have heard something by now. It was taking too long. She looked at her watch again.
- ★ She looked down at her watch. They'd got less than an hour. Time was running out.
- ★ There was less than five minutes to go.
- ★ The monitor was flashing. The countdown clock displayed 20 seconds.
- ★ *They weren't going to make it in time.*
- ★ But he was too late, far too late.
- ★ He was too slow, and one second too late before the gates slammed shut.

A DECISION/PLAN

* ★ He knew his next move would be crucial. He ran through his options.
* ★ His rescue plan relied on stealth, cunning and a great deal of luck.
* ★ He felt hopeless, but going back would be admitting defeat. It was time to fight back.
* ★ He was about to give up hope when . . .
* ★ All the pieces were fitting together. She was beginning to form a plan and was ready to fight hard to stay alive.
* ★ Suddenly, out of nowhere he had an idea. He knew what he needed to do next and he knew he was taking a huge risk. But he had no other choice.
* ★ It was then that she knew what she had to do. There was nothing left to lose.
* ★ She was convinced that they had reached yet another dead end. Suddenly, a light flashed in her head; a searchlight cutting through the dark maze. A jolt of memory.
* ★ Somewhere, buried deep in her memory, she had a feeling she should know that name.
* ★ The breakthrough, when it eventually arrived, came from an unexpected source.
* ★ Whatever had happened in that house was the key to the mystery.
* ★ There was something about the man – the way he was looking at her, the way his eyes flickered briefly. This man knew something.
* ★ She felt there was an answer there – a vital piece of information she needed.
* ★ He was convinced that the old tramp was the key to solving the mystery.
* ★ Then came an incredible piece of luck.
* ★ But a moment later, salvation, unexpected and unimagined, appeared through the night.
* ★ She thought back to something the old man had said.
* ★ *It was all beginning to make sense at last.*
* ★ With a jolt like an electric shock, he finally understood.
* ★ Suddenly, she knew they were on to something big.
* ★ In a split second, he realised what was happening.
* ★ Just when he was thinking of giving up . . . He strolled to the hearth. In the embers, he discovered a singed map. He blew out the glowing embers and studied the outline.

WHAT'S LURKING BEHIND THE DOOR?

* ★ He jumped as the door swung open.
* ★ A pool of dim light leaked through the door as it was edged open and a hand reached out.
* ★ He glanced up to see the door handle turning.
* ★ She heard the door handle turn and sensed a body enter the room.

* A key turned in the door. He dropped to his knees. The door creaked open . . . slowly opened wider. A figure was silhouetted in the doorway.
* He opened his eyes. He scanned the room to find the source of the noise that had woken him. Then he turned and saw what had disturbed him. In the doorway of the room stood . . .
* He heard a key turn in the lock. There was no time to lose. He had to get out of there.
* *The door opened with a quiet click.*
* The door made a sharp screech as someone tried to pull it open, snapping the chain taut.
* The door glided open with a soft shushing sound.
* The door banged shut behind him with a booming finality.
* Suddenly, the bolt securing his door snapped back with a metallic clank, and the hinges squealed like nails on chalkboard.
* She heard the squeak of a door handle, the groan of the hinges and the creak of footsteps on the floorboards.
* *Without stopping to think what might be on the other side, he opened the door and slipped through.*
* Opening the door to his room, he stopped dead in his tracks.
* Her hopes were dashed as soon as she turned the handle.
* She knew that she should move and search for a door on the other side of the corridor, but she was afraid to move, afraid of what was on the other side.
* *A low mumble of voices was coming from behind the door.*
* Pressing their ears to the door, they listened carefully for any sound in the room. Another minute passed, and still they heard nothing.
* For several moments they huddled together in the dark, holding their breath, and straining their ears for any noises on the other side of the door.

TOO CLOSE FOR COMFORT

* That had been close, too close. If he had been caught it would have all been over for him.
* The footsteps were louder. Another creak from down the corridor. Only seconds away.
* At that moment, she heard footsteps outside the door.
* Any second now, they would be discovered. Every moment they delayed, the footsteps were moving closer.
* He heard the muffled sound of feet pursuing him through the snow.
* The footsteps were getting closer. Whoever it was had almost reached the top of the stairs. In seconds, they would be close enough to see him.
* The steps seemed to be moving away from where he was concealed, but then, in a moment of utter terror, he heard voices behind him. They had circled round and were now on his side of the track.

* Outside, he heard the clump of boots on the stairs and a moment later, a heavy fist thudded on his door.
* He heard the thundering boots of men on the stairs behind him.
* The footsteps were growing louder and getting closer. He could hear the squeak of boot leather.
* *As he crouched in the ditch, he could hear the voices of the men close by in the shadows ahead of him.*
* Behind him, the guards were calling softly to each other.
* Suddenly, the breeze carried the murmur of her name.
* He was over halfway when the sound of voices alerted him to danger.
* After following the tunnel for a while, they heard hushed voices close by.
* He heard a voice whispering in the room, and he was aware that there was someone – or something – standing very close to him.
* Then she heard something nearby, the slightest catch of breath.
* Nearer and nearer they came until he could hear their breathing.
* The shouts behind him grew louder and closer.
* *A noise, close behind him, made him turn.*
* It was a very soft thud, barely audible even in the absolute silence.
* He became aware of faint, muffled sounds of movement.
* Then he heard a sound – the quiet, stealthy sound of someone moving.
* He heard a movement in the house. Somebody had arrived. He could hear voices, radios crackling.
* A flicker of sound from the darkness caught her ear.
* Just then she heard something. She was on her feet immediately, crouching down. She heard another sound. The single crack of a branch breaking.
* They heard the snap of twigs. Someone was moving very fast through the wood, towards them, not caring where they put their feet.
* *The sound of the engines grew gradually louder.*
* They heard the crunch of wheels close at hand, and stepped back into the shadow of the pillar.
* That's when he heard the unmistakable whooping beat of a fast-approaching helicopter.
* The helicopters were getting closer. She could hear the whirr of the blades.
* *Suddenly, to his horror, a torch beam passed over his outstretched hand.*
* There was a rattle of a key in the lock and the door opened, bathing the room in light.
* A hand reached out in the dim light, searching for the switch. Her nose started to twitch. She tried to swallow the sneeze. She pressed her fist into her mouth as she felt the sneeze threatening to explode. The hand stopped moving. Then a bright light pierced the gloom, swinging from side to side.

2

The journey

WORDS

Nouns	**Adventure**, journey
	Mountains, slopes, forest, woods, swamps, rivers
Adjectives	**Long**, difficult
	Dense, impenetrable, sheer, rushing
	Alert
Verbs	**Travelled**, journeyed
	Climbed, crossed
	Trekked, trudged, tramped, plodded, stumbled, struggled, scrambled

---

PHRASES – NOUNS AND ADJECTIVES

★ Long journey
★ Difficult journey
★ All the way to . . .
★ Miles and miles
★ In the distance . . .
★ *Every day* . . .
★ For a week . . .
★ Hours before they . . .
★ For the next hour . . .
★ *Mostly by night*
★ Through the night
★ Blackest depths of the night

PHRASES – VERBS

- ☆ Going to be a long journey
- ☆ Would take them across . . .
- ☆ Travelled through . . .
- ☆ *Would have to climb mountains*
- ☆ Struggle through swamps
- ☆ Cross raging rivers
- ☆ Find a way through dense, impenetrable forests
- ☆ Faced with new problems and challenges
- ☆ *Journeyed mostly by night*
- ☆ Guided by the moon
- ☆ Found a place to hide
- ☆ Crept into the woods
- ☆ Slept under the trees
- ☆ *Moved up the trail*
- ☆ Reached the top
- ☆ Entered the jungle
- ☆ *Trudged on in silence*
- ☆ Had to push on
- ☆ Sucked every ounce of energy out of them
- ☆ Reached their destination

SENTENCES

They realised that somehow their old life had ended and a new one was about to begin. It was an adventure that would take them across . . . all the way to . . .

Wherever she was going, it was going to be a long journey.

They knew they would have to climb mountains, struggle through swamps, cross rushing rivers, and find a way through dense, impenetrable forest before they eventually reached their destination.

Their journey was difficult, and every day they were faced with new problems.

For a week, she travelled on, journeying mostly by night.

He had travelled through the blackest depths of the night, stumbling on, constantly alert for any sound or movement.

Guided by the moon, they travelled all night.

Kitty trudged on wearily for miles and miles until she heard the sound of the river.

He knew he had to push on during the night and find a place to hide during the daylight.

12 *The journey*

They crept into the woods during the night and slept under the trees.

Shouldering her rucksack, she moved up the trail, glancing up every so often to see how far she still had to climb before she reached the top.

They went miles and miles down the steep slope before they entered the jungle.

They trudged on – silent, as exhaustion sucked every ounce of energy out of them. How different things would have been if they had turned back.

For the next hour, he stumbled on, every muscle burning with exhaustion, and then, there in the distance, he saw it. Falling to his knees, he buried his head in his hands, unable to believe that he had actually made it.

3
Routes

SECTION 1 – CITIES, TOWNS AND VILLAGES

WORDS	
Nouns	**Roads**, streets, lanes, alleys, passageways, town square, high street
	Buildings, restaurants, shops, entrance
	Tube station, stairs, platform
	Traffic, buses, lorries, cars, bikes, crowds
	Tunnels, cellars, maze, warren, labyrinth
	Bend, corner
Adjectives	**Busy**, noisy, dirty, dark
	Secret, underground, cobbled
	Narrow, steep, sheer, high
	Twisting, winding, hairpin
	Sinister, dangerous, perilous, terrifying
	Potholed, bone-shaking, dusty
Verbs	**Jammed**, clogged, jostled
	Led, blocked
	Bent, twisted, turned, curved, coiled, crabbed
	Struck, shook, shuddered, sprayed

PHRASES – NOUNS AND ADJECTIVES

★ Good place to hide
★ *Dark, narrow alley*
★ Cobbled alleyway
★ Warren of narrow, twisting alleys
★ Labyrinth of secret, underground tunnels and cellars
★ Maze of buildings
★ Passage at the back of the restaurants
★ Sinister shadows on the ground in front of him
★ *High walls*
★ Coils of barbed wire
★ Piles of boxes and rubbish
★ *Hairpin bends*
★ Canyon walls
★ Terrifyingly sheer drop
★ Steep descent
★ Dizzying drop beneath him
★ *Potholed road*
★ Clouds of dust

PHRASES – VERBS

★ Found themselves walking down . . .
★ Clogged with traffic
★ *Jostled their way forward*
★ Dodged the traffic
★ Ran across the city
★ Turned off the main high street
★ Ducked into side streets
★ Darted into shops
★ Dived inside
★ Hurled down the stairs
★ Disappeared underground
★ *Used to move around the city*
★ Blocked the road
★ Topped with coils of barbed wire
★ *Twisted and turned*
★ Crabbed along the mountain
★ Started downwards in a steep descent
★ *Shuddered along the road*
★ Leapt into the air
★ Struck the huge potholes
★ Sprayed the windscreen

SENTENCES

Lots of alleyways led off from the town square.

The town was a warren of tunnels, narrow, twisting alleys and a maze of buildings.

They ran across the city, dodging the traffic, ducking into side roads, darting into shops . . . doing everything they could to make sure they weren't being followed. Eventually, they found an entrance to a tube station and hurled down the stairs, disappearing underground. There was a train on the platform. Not caring where it was going, they dived inside.

Morning and night, the roads were clogged with traffic: buses, lorries, cars and bikes, noisily jostling their way forward. It was a good place to hide in the crowd, but harder to spot anyone following him.

The passage at the back of the restaurants was so narrow he could have stretched out his arms and touched both walls at once. Piles of boxes and rubbish blocked the way.

They turned off the main high street. Suddenly, they found themselves walking down a narrow, cobbled alleyway between two high walls topped with coils of barbed wire, which cast sinister shadows on the ground in front of them.

Hundreds of years before, the warren of secret, underground tunnels and cellars had been used to move around the city and to hide from invaders in times of danger. He couldn't think of a better place to stay out of sight until he was ready to make his move.

The road started downwards in a steep descent and crabbed along the mountain in a series of perilous curves, twisting and turning like a coiled spring.

The car shuddered along the bone-shaking trail. Clouds of dust sprayed the windscreen and the car leaped into the air as the front tyres struck the potholes.

The road snaked through a dozen hairpin bends. To the left of the road, the canyon wall was so close he could have leaned out of the car and touched it. To the right, there was a terrifyingly sheer drop.

SECTION 2 – PATHS AND TRAILS

WORDS

Nouns	**Track**, trail, path, terrain
	Marshes, forest, woodland, trees, branches, thicket, thorns
	Mountain, cliff, rock, boulders, stones, ravine, tunnel
	Bridge, river, stream, waterfall, rapids, cascades

Adjectives	**Forgotten**, ancient, secret
	Narrow, winding, twisting
	Large, small
	Thick, impenetrable, dark, shadowy
	Huge, towering
	Rugged, ankle-twisting, fast-flowing
Verbs	**Searched**, glimpsed
	Began, led, ran, followed, carved, wound, twisted, turned, coiled, ended
	Hidden, buried
	Climbed, dipped, dropped, plummeted
	Battled, clambered, scrambled, leaped

PHRASES – NOUNS AND ADJECTIVES

* No obvious trail
* Forgotten path
* *Narrow, winding track*
* Ancient track
* Secret paths through the marshes
* *Along a narrow road*
* Through an opening in the trees
* Through the shadowy darkness
* *Thick woodland*
* Snarls of vines and shrubs
* Towering trees
* Huge branches
* Impenetrable, thorny thickets
* *Huge, towering cliff*
* Wall of rock
* Rugged terrain
* Ankle-twisting boulders
* Fields of loose stones
* Narrow ravine
* Through a tunnel
* Hissing avalanche of stones
* *Humpbacked bridge*
* Small footbridge
* *Series of crashing cascades*
* Banks of the fast-flowing river

PHRASES – VERBS

 * ⭐ Searched for a way forward
 * ⭐ Came across a forgotten path
 * ⭐ Caught a brief glimpse of . . .
 * ⭐ *Led deep into the forest*
 * ⭐ Plummeted into the woods
 * ⭐ Led away to the east
 * ⭐ Led down to some shadowy steps
 * ⭐ *Carved its way through . . .*
 * ⭐ Began to zigzag
 * ⭐ *Became more and more overgrown*
 * ⭐ Lost in the brambles
 * ⭐ Hidden by thorns and creepers
 * ⭐ Buried deep in a ditch between the hedges
 * ⭐ Swallowed up by darkness
 * ⭐ *Coiled round the mountain*
 * ⭐ Climbed steeply up the side of the mountain
 * ⭐ Ended in a wall of rock
 * ⭐ *Battled his way through . . .*
 * ⭐ Made their way over . . .
 * ⭐ Wound their way down the mountain
 * ⭐ Scrambled up . . .
 * ⭐ Clambered over . . .
 * ⭐ *Crossed the river*
 * ⭐ Helped each other scale the stones
 * ⭐ Leaped off on the other side
 * ⭐ Covered in green slimy fungus

SENTENCES

There was no obvious trail. He had to battle his way through snarls of vines and shrubs.

They made their way over a humpbacked bridge and along a narrow road that carved its way through thick woodland.

Their way lay on secret paths through the marshes that only those who knew they existed could have found.

Through an opening in the trees, he caught a brief glimpse of a narrow track that led away to the east.

He searched for a way forward, until finally he came across what seemed to be a forgotten path, hidden by thorns and creepers and leading deep into the forest, where it was quickly swallowed up by darkness.

The ancient track began to zigzag around impenetrable, thorny thickets. It was impossible to see more than ten paces ahead through the shadowy darkness created by the towering trees that spread their huge branches to block out the light.

The muddy track led up into the forest, and for much of its winding way it was buried deep in a ditch between the hedges.

There was no path, so to reach the top they had to scramble up craggy rocks and clamber over huge boulders.

He clambered up on a bank of rock, then doubled back through a tunnel and squeezed through a hidden gap that led towards a narrow ravine.

He climbed up the ravine until he reached the upper edge, where he commando-crawled behind a large clump of gorse.

The terrain was rugged, with ankle-twisting boulders and fields of loose stones that could be dislodged into a hissing avalanche with an ill-placed boot. They moved cautiously, always glancing behind them for any sign of movement.

When they got there, they were confronted with a huge, towering cliff, a wall of rock. A river flowed down the surface of this cliff in a series of crashing cascades. They had come to a dead end!

They followed the course of the mountain stream as it rushed downhill, until they came to a small footbridge and could cross over the stream to where the trail led into the forest.

If they were to continue travelling south, they would have to cross the river. The smooth stones over which the river gushed were covered in slimy green fungus.

They helped each other scale the stones, leaped off on the other side, wound their way down the mountain towards the banks of the fast-flowing river.

SECTION 3 – GROUND

A. Dry ground

WORDS	
Nouns	**Hillside**, ground, earth
	Potholes, cracks, leaves, twigs
Adjectives	**Red**, brown, dry, dusty, baked, arid, scorched, parched, barren
	Treacherous, steep, deep
Verbs	**Cracked**, burned, roasted, withered

PHRASES – NOUNS AND ADJECTIVES

* ★ Dry, baked, red ground
* ★ Enormous cracks in the scorched earth
* ★ Ground was as dry as cork underfoot
* ★ Withered, dead leaves and fallen twigs
* ★ Dry like the skin of an old elephant
* ★ Treacherous potholes

PHRASES – VERBS

* ★ Roasted by the sun
* ★ Appeared in the ground
* ★ Blew a cloud of dust along the road
* ★ Crunched on the withered, dead leaves

SENTENCES

The land was barren. Nothing grew on the dry, baked, red ground.

The months without rain had caused enormous cracks to appear in the scorched earth.

The ground was as dry as cork underfoot and her feet crunched on the withered, dead leaves and fallen twigs.

The steep turf was dotted with deep, treacherous potholes.

B. Wet ground

WORDS

Nouns	**Bog**, marsh, swamp
	Moss, lichen, leaf-mould, mud
Adjectives	**Wet**, muddy, swampy, boggy, waterlogged, slippery, squelchy, slimy, gooey
	Stiffened
Verbs	**Fell**, slipped, skidded, scrambled, struggled, sank
	Swallowed, held, clung, sucked, clawed, wrenched
	Crunched, squelched

PHRASES – NOUNS AND ADJECTIVES

* ★ Like muddy soup
* ★ Shimmering, silver bogs
* ★ Squelching, slimy mud
* ★ Slippery moss and lichen
* ★ Wet, slippery, leaf-mould and mud
* ★ Layers of thick, wet mud
* ★ Thick clods
* ★ Gooey slime
* ★ Persistent, sucking grip
* ★ Beneath his boots

PHRASES – VERBS

* ★ Swallowed her feet
* ★ Clung all the way up to her ankles
* ★ Held her in its squelching, slimy grasp
* ★ Struggled to gain a foothold
* ★ Slipped and clawed her way through the gooey slime
* ★ Fell back in a mud-slide
* ★ Could barely lift his legs free of the ooze
* ★ Sank up to her knees in mud

SENTENCES

The ground sucked at his boots.

The stiffened mud crunched beneath his boots.

The ground was like muddy soup and swallowed her feet in its squelching, slimy grasp.

She scrambled up the vertical bank, which was slimy with damp leaf-mould and mud.

He struggled to gain a foothold on the slippery moss and lichen, slicing his fingers on the crumbling ridges of the stone wall.

Skidding across layers of thick, wet mud, she clawed her way through the gooey slime, and came within centimetres of the top, only to fall back in the wake of a mud-slide.

Mud squelched in hungry sucks as each foot was wrenched from its persistent grip.

When he lifted his foot from the muck, thick clods clung all the way to his ankle and every step he seemed to collect more. After just a few paces, he could barely lift his legs free of the ooze.

C. Cold ground

WORDS

Nouns	**Frost**, ice, snow
Adjectives	**Hard**, frozen, solid, black, white
Verbs	**Groaned**, cracked, split, glinted, gleamed
	Seeped

PHRASES – NOUNS AND ADJECTIVES

* Glittering ice
* Hard with black frost
* White frost in the shadows

PHRASES – VERBS

* Glinted with frost
* Cracked and crunched
* Groaned and cracked
* Split like a lightning bolt
* Seeped through his boots

SENTENCES

The ground was covered in frost and glinted dangerously.

The earth was hard with black frost that seeped through his sodden boots and spread ice into every limb.

Below his feet, the glittering ice cracked and groaned.

White frost gleamed in the shadows – cold and dangerous.

They were surrounded by ice, which groaned and cracked until, finally, it split like a lightning bolt.

4

Moving closer to the destination

1. **Something was very wrong. He could feel it. A tingling sixth sense of danger lurking in the shadows. He tensed.** The red light on the movement detector flickered as it sensed him. Before he had reached the end of the corridor, sirens shattered the silence with their urgent, high-pitched shrieking.

2. **As a surge of adrenalin shot through her, every nerve in Katie's body was on high alert.** She picked a large weed and crawled nearer, throwing it so that it leaned against the fence. She waited, **holding her breath**. Then she heard it – a buzzing noise. It was an electric fence!

3. The bridge sagged in the middle and looked ready to collapse, but it was now the only way to get across. As he walked onto the bridge, it started to wobble. The others urged him on, and he edged cautiously out towards the middle, his **eyes firmly fixed on the other side, his palms sweating as he clung to the guide rope**. Suddenly, the bridge began to sway like a pendulum. **Paralysed by fear, he was rooted to the spot, unable to turn back, too scared to move forward!**

4. **Senses fully alert**, they advanced, hunched over in a crouch, and vaulted over the fence. **Tom had the distinct feeling they were being watched** from one of the upper windows. **Sweat broke out on the palms of his hands and he had to keep rubbing them dry on his trousers.**

5. **A tight knot in the pit of her stomach warned Gail she was walking into trouble. Shuddering, she fought back the urge to flee.** She eased down the handle a fraction at a time; stopped a moment and listened. The rusty

hinges hadn't squeaked. She opened it a bit more, unsure of what she would discover inside.

SECTION 1 – SETTING

A. Barriers

WORDS	
Nouns	**Ditches**, moat, trench, ground, potholes, bomb crater
	Bridge, wall, gate, fence, fencing, wire, barbs, spikes
Adjectives	**Brick**, stone, wooden, metal, steel, iron, wrought iron
	Chain-link, mesh, coiled, barbed, electric, buzzing, fortified
	Sliding, five-barred
Verbs	**Surrounded**, spanned, set back, towered
	Protected, stationed
	Sagged, wobbled, swayed

PHRASES – NOUNS AND ADJECTIVES

- ★ At the end of the tarmac road . . .
- ★ On the other side, he could see . . .
- ★ *Two-metre-high wall*
- ★ Massive fortified walls
- ★ Another wall, another dead end, no escape
- ★ Brick wall, several metres high, with razor wire around the top
- ★ *Deep defensive ditches*
- ★ Narrow drainage ditch
- ★ Trench in the ground
- ★ Potholes the size of bomb craters
- ★ Slopes of sliding stones and boulders
- ★ *Wire fence*
- ★ Chain-link fence
- ★ High-security fencing
- ★ A double line of ten-foot-high chain-link fence
- ★ *Barbed wire*
- ★ Coiled barbed wire in the space between
- ★ Razor wire
- ★ Spikes on top of the wrought iron fence

★ Barbs of steel like vicious daggers
★ Buzzing noise of an electric fence
★ Electrified perimeter fence
★ *Sliding gate, heavily guarded*
★ Huge metal gates
★ Grille gate in the wall
★ Heavy five-barred gate
★ Burly sentries
★ *Rope bridge*
★ Like the bridge was suspended in thin air
★ A narrow landing strip of rock
★ *Only way to get across*
★ Only the mist ahead of them

PHRASES – VERBS

★ *Surrounded by . . .*
★ Set back behind
★ Towered in front of her
★ Could just make out
★ Strung along the top
★ Stationed at every door
★ Spanned a thirty-metre chasm
★ *Opened with a metallic clank*
★ Started to swing inwards
★ Rattled as some invisible bolt was released
★ Opened automatically with a remote control system
★ Bristled with cameras
★ Sent long shadows streaking from the buildings
★ Heard the buzzing noise
★ Knew that the fence had been electrified
★ *Gazed up at the huge metal gates*
★ Crawled near the fence
★ *Straddled the wall with ease*
★ Swung her trailing leg over swiftly
★ Landed on the opposite side
★ *Plucked a weed near his right hand*
★ Threw it so that it leaned against the fence
★ *Was the only way to cross*
★ Could not see the end of the bridge
★ Covered in a cloud of mist
★ Sagged in the middle
★ Looked ready to collapse

* *Swayed like a pendulum*
* Began to wobble
* *Led out onto the summit*
* Opened into some sort of underground storage area

SENTENCES

The property was like an ancient fortress, surrounded by deep, defensive ditches and massive fortified walls.

A line of high chain-link fence, topped with coiled barbed wire, formed an impenetrable barrier.

Beyond the wall, the ground was peppered with potholes the size of bomb craters. These would present a real danger of twisting an ankle or worse if they attempted to get across at night.

Looking through the gaps in the trees, they could see a high metal fence. They wouldn't dare to scale it until they knew whether or not it had been electrified. It looked harmless enough.

Rob picked a large weed and crawled near the fence. He threw it so that it leaned against the fence. They waited, holding their breath. Then they heard it – a buzzing noise. It was an electric fence!

The gate was opened automatically by a remote control system. They would have to wait until it opened to let a car in or out and try to sneak past the sentries.

To get to the caves, they had to cross a rope bridge, which looked as if it was suspended in thin air. They could not see the other end. It was covered in a cloud of mist.

The bridge sagged in the middle and looked ready to collapse, but it was now the only way to get across.

B. Alarms

WORDS

Nouns   **Alarm**, sensor, scanner, detectors, lock, panel, console, switch, button

Camera, floodlights, searchlights, movement detectors, CCTV cameras, siren, buzzer, trip-wire, booby trap

Building, entrance, corner

Beep, shriek, howl

Adjectives	**Small**, slight, thin
	Red, white
	Shrill, high-pitched, piercing, whooping, deafening
Verbs	**Reached**, passed
	Gazed, watched, spotted, heard
	Swept, lit, sliced, broke, filled
	Howled, shrieked, clattered, jangled
	Sounded, echoed, slammed, shattered
	Set off, flickered, indicated
	Placed, tied, concealed, designed
	Poised, pushed

PHRASES – NOUNS AND ADJECTIVES

- ★ On the sides of each building
- ★ A few inches from his face
- ★ Just above ground level
- ★ Scarcely visible
- ★ *Signs of a security system*
- ★ Sophisticated cameras
- ★ CCTV cameras above the entrance
- ★ Infrared sensors
- ★ *An alarm button*
- ★ On one of the control panels
- ★ A small console containing a series of red switches
- ★ X-ray scanners, a metal detector and guards
- ★ Red light on the movement detector
- ★ *No warning tone*
- ★ A silent alarm
- ★ Slight beep as the lock was activated
- ★ Warning buzzers
- ★ Deafening alarm
- ★ High-pitched siren
- ★ Urgent shrieking
- ★ Shrill, piercing alarm
- ★ Whooping like an ambulance siren
- ★ *Metal shutters*
- ★ *Series of searchlights*
- ★ Brilliant light

- ★ *Laser trip-wire*
- ★ Thin strand of nylon wire
- ★ Booby trap
- ★ Line of bottles

PHRASES – VERBS

- ★ Reached for an alarm switch
- ★ *Gazed down from every angle*
- ★ Placed above the entrance
- ★ Watched every movement
- ★ Flickered as it sensed him
- ★ Passed through one of them
- ★ *Heard a slight beep*
- ★ Lock was activated
- ★ Indicated that the door had been opened
- ★ *Set off a . . .*
- ★ Broke the silence
- ★ Jangling along the corridor
- ★ Followed by the sound of . . .
- ★ Echoed around him
- ★ Filled the air
- ★ Filled the room
- ★ Began to wail
- ★ Began to howl
- ★ Swept through the air
- ★ Shattered the silence
- ★ Shrieking everywhere
- ★ Going off all over the compound
- ★ Metal shutters slammed down
- ★ *Lit up the area*
- ★ Sliced through the darkness
- ★ *Spotted a wire*
- ★ Tied between two trees
- ★ *Designed to alert the main house*
- ★ Concealed at the entrance to . . .
- ★ Triggered a silent alarm
- ★ Poised precariously on the rim of a stool
- ★ Pushed up against the door
- ★ Clattered to the stone floor as the door was edged open

SENTENCES

He looked up and saw CCTV cameras above the entrance.

Dozens of cameras jutted out on each of the walls, gazing down from every angle, watching his every move.

He heard a slight beep that indicated that the door had been opened. Thirty seconds later, a siren began to wail throughout the building.

As he passed through the metal detector, warning buzzers sounded and he saw the guard's fingers moving towards the alarm button concealed under the desk. An alarm started to wail.

The red light on the movement sensor flickered as it sensed him.

Without warning, a spotlight swept over the front of the building and the metal shutter slammed down.

He tensed as he spotted the red light on the movement detector flickering as it sensed him. Before he had reached the end of the corridor, sirens shattered the silence with their urgent, high-pitched shrieking.

The whole area exploded into a brilliant white light, which sliced through the darkness and caught him in its glaring beam.

Cautiously, he probed the ground in front of him. Suddenly, he spotted a thin strand of nylon wire tied between two trees just above ground level. It was designed to alert the security guards to any intruders.

Three glass bottles had been placed on the edge of a stool that had been pushed against the door. As soon as the door was opened from the outside, the bottles would topple, clatter onto the stone floor and smash.

SECTION 2 – INTERACTION

A. Scanning the area

WORDS

Nouns	**Darkness**, shadows
	Look, gaze, glimpse, signal, movement, direction
	Head, eyes
	Horizon, landscape, countryside, area, scene, crowd
	Trees, branches, undergrowth, bushes, reeds
	Alleyway, street, entrance, arcade, wall, building, door
	Vantage point, look-out post, guards, sentry

Adjectives	**Immediate**, brief, fleeting
	Still, motionless, anxious, alert
Verbs	**Looked**, watched, scanned, searched, stared, strained
	Glanced, roamed, swept, flitted, peeked
	Moved, turned, twisted
	Stopped, waited, retreated

PHRASES – NOUNS AND ADJECTIVES

* ★ For the hundredth time
* ★ *The path ahead*
* ★ On the other side
* ★ On top of the hill
* ★ Across the roof from their position
* ★ Outside the door
* ★ *Security barrier*
* ★ Iron gates
* ★ *Trail of footprints*
* ★ Flicker of movement
* ★ Moving specks
* ★ *Long rows of cars and empty spaces*

PHRASES – VERBS

* ★ Scanned the horizon anxiously
* ★ Scanned the surrounding countryside
* ★ Searched the immediate area
* ★ Watched the crowds
* ★ Swept the scene in front of him
* ★ Scanned the darkness
* ★ *Settled down on his stomach to watch . . .*
* ★ Elbowed himself up into a sitting position
* ★ Watched from his vantage point
* ★ Peered through . . .
* ★ Retreated further into the shadows
* ★ *Gazed up at the edge of the forest*
* ★ Stared at the door
* ★ Watched the entrance
* ★ Squinted in the direction of . . .
* ★ Looked furtively up and down the . . .
* ★ Allowed her gaze to rake from end to end

* *Waiting for a signal*
* Searched for any movement
* Made sure the coast was clear
* Looked left and right
* Stared up and down . . .
* Turned his head frequently
* Flitted from one direction to the next
* Peeked over the wall
* Caught a glimpse of . . .

He looked left and right anxiously. There was nobody else around.

Katie settled down on her stomach and scanned the surrounding area.

They looked up and down the street for the hundredth time.

She looked both ways to check that the coast was clear.

He scanned the darkness, the trees and bushes on either side of the track, watching for the least movement.

As he scanned the crowds, Tom caught a glimpse of two figures emerging from the arcade.

Darting forward, Katie kept low and threw herself down on the top of the hill behind the trees so that she could look down without being spotted.

Tom stared at the entrance to the building, allowing his gaze to rake from end to end, making sure that everyone had left.

He watched from his vantage point on the top of the hill as the lights in the houses went out one by one and the village was slowly steeped in darkness.

For several nights, he observed the routes and routine of the security patrols.

He watched and waited. Slowly, he peered out and squinted into the darkness. His eyes darted left and right, probing the forest for a flicker of movement.

B. Signals

WORDS

Nouns	**Head**, eyes, lips
	Shoulders, arms, hands, fist, fingers
	Look, glance, sign, signal, movement, jerk

Shadow, bushes, house, fire-escape, door, stairs, corridor, windows

Adjectives	**Backwards**, rearwards, forwards, upwards, downwards, sideways
	Still, motionless, anxious, alert
Verbs	**Looked**, scanned, glanced, shot, locked
	Communicated, indicated, mimed, motioned, gestured, beckoned, gesticulated, nodded
	Lifted, held up, raised, outstretched
	Pointed, waved, shook
	Stood, moved, ducked, followed, ran
	Pressed, pulled, spread
	Warned, pleaded, quietened
Adverbs	**Vigorously**, feverishly
	Slowly, cautiously, stealthily, furtively
	Quietly, silently

PHRASES – NOUNS AND ADJECTIVES

- ★ *Sign language*
- ★ Silent cue
- ★ System of arm signals
- ★ *Silent look of warning*
- ★ Warning glance
- ★ *Out of the corner of her eye*
- ★ Into the distance
- ★ *Length of the corridor*
- ★ Along the corridor
- ★ Out of the room
- ★ Under the windows
- ★ Around the side of the house
- ★ Shadow of the tree

PHRASES – VERBS

- ★ Communicated only with sign language
- ★ *Raised a fist*
- ★ Spread her arms

★ Waved his arms
★ Mimed a lip-zipping action
★ *Shook her head*
★ Jerked his head
★ *Shot her a look*
★ Looked over his shoulder
★ *Told them to split up*
★ Pleaded with her to keep still
★ Motioned for them to stop
★ Beckoned for him to follow
★ Urged them to run
★ *Warned her not to make a sound*
★ Waved an arm to quieten them
★ Held up his hand for silence
★ Motioned for her to be silent
★ *Raised his hand to signal danger*
★ Pointed down the . . .
★ Indicated the entrance
★ Go around the . . .
★ Gestured behind him
★ Hide in the bushes
★ Gesticulated upwards with his fingers
★ *Scanned the courtyard*
★ Pulled her into the shadows

SENTENCES

Tom indicated the entrance with a rearward jerk of his head.

Katie looked over her shoulder at him and put a finger to her lips, warning him to be quiet.

When he raised his hand to signal someone was coming, the others immediately ducked down low.

Out of the corner of her eye, Katie saw something hidden in the shadows. Something that had not been there before. She glanced at Tom and shot him a warning glance to keep hidden.

As he rose up to peer over the wall, Katie gestured for him to get down and pointed silently into the distance.

Signalling with his hands, he warned her that from then on they could only communicate with sign language. She nodded.

With his arm outstretched, Alfie pointed down to the end of the tunnel. He looked over his shoulder, silently urging them to run back.

C. Advancing

WORDS	

Nouns	**Minutes**, hours, eternity
	Senses, sound, noises
	Silence, whispers, rustles, squawks, footsteps
	Darkness, shadow, light, torch
	Movement, pace, direction
	Path, fence, gate, courtyard, house, building, entrance, door, wall, window, corner, CCTV cameras, floodlights
	Ground, undergrowth, trench, ditch, tree, branch, bushes, reeds
	Cave, tunnel, passages, slope, gap
	Hands, knees, shoulder, feet
Adjectives	**Cautious**, alert
Verbs	**Climbed**, clambered, hoisted, sprung, leapt, launched, vaulted, straddled, landed
	Crawled, crept, wriggled, slithered, commando-crawled, rolled, writhed, twisted
	Moved, inched, edged, eased, stepped, shuffled
	Felt, touched
	Stopped, waited, paused, halted, hesitated, checked
	Slipped, shifted, skirted
	Hugged, brushed, pressed
	Looked, peered, strained, shone
	Quickened, ran, sprinted, scampered, scurried
Adverbs	**Cautiously**, carefully, gingerly, quietly
	Quickly, swiftly

PHRASES – NOUNS AND ADJECTIVES	

- ★ For what seemed like an eternity
- ★ For a few minutes
- ★ *Senses fully alert*

* More cautious
* *As though they were part of the mist*
* Like soldiers crossing no-man's land
* As quickly and as quietly as possible
* *Careful of their footing*
* Nearly at a full run
* In one swift movement
* *In the direction of . . .*
* On the other side of . . .
* *Towards the house*
* Back of the building
* Wall straight ahead of them
* Top of the wall
* Side window
* Shadow of the neighbouring courtyard
* *Through the undergrowth*
* Clumps of reeds
* Behind the tree
* *Dark tunnels*
* Through a warren of passages
* Up a steep slope
* *Night-vision goggles*

PHRASES – VERBS

* *Climbed up the . . .*
* Poised to leap
* Hoisted her up to the . . .
* Made a stirrup with his hands
* *Sprung upwards*
* Vaulted the fence
* Eased himself over . . .
* Clambered over . . .
* Leaped over the side of . . .
* Launched himself over the fence
* *Pushed his trainers against the sill of a lower window*
* *Leapt down onto the . . .*
* Climbed down into the trench
* Landed in a crouch
* Curled herself into a ball
* Rose up from his haunches
* *Crept to the wall on hands and knees*
* Crept cautiously through the reeds

- ☆ Wriggled through the undergrowth
- ☆ Crawled underneath the . . .
- ☆ Slithered on their bellies
- ☆ Commando-crawled as close as he dared
- ☆ Rolled onto his side
- ☆ Rolled rapidly across . . .
- ☆ Writhing and twisting, crawled through the gap
- ☆ Hunched over, he moved forward
- ☆ *Inched closer*
- ☆ Inched towards the . . .
- ☆ Eased through the . . .
- ☆ Edged deeper into the darkness
- ☆ Moved one foot in front of the other
- ☆ Felt her way along
- ☆ Felt his way cautiously
- ☆ Touched the sides of the tunnel with one hand
- ☆ Shuffled quickly sideways
- ☆ Shuffled blindly in the direction of . . .
- ☆ Stepped gingerly to the edge of . . .
- ☆ Moved in stages, one moving, the other still
- ☆ *Scanned, checked – constantly alert*
- ☆ Moved in total silence
- ☆ Spoke in whispers
- ☆ *Shone her torch*
- ☆ Checked what lay ahead with his torch
- ☆ *Stayed in the blind spots of the CCTV cameras*
- ☆ Emerged from the shadow of the gateway
- ☆ *Halted at every rustle and squawk*
- ☆ Waited before he moved again
- ☆ Waited a moment and then followed
- ☆ Paused on the other side
- ☆ Made sure no one had heard the noise
- ☆ Paused . . . nothing stirred . . . moved on
- ☆ Paused frequently to listen for unnatural sounds
- ☆ Began to move forward . . . paused again
- ☆ Hesitated outside the entrance to the cave
- ☆ Stopped and dropped into a crouch
- ☆ Listened underneath the window . . .
- ☆ *Slipped around the side*
- ☆ Worked his way down the path
- ☆ Shifted round the house to the front door
- ☆ Skirted the . . .
- ☆ Moved to the corner of . . .
- ☆ Approached the back of . . .

* Skirted the rear of . . .
* Worked his way through the . . .
* Moved along the walls
* Hugged the wall
* Brushed his shoulder against the walls
* Pressed himself against the wall
* Kept close to the shadows
* Searched for another entrance
* *Peered inside*
* Peered over the wall
* Peered over the edge
* Peered furtively around corners
* Strained his neck to peer upwards
* Leaned forward just enough to see around the . . .
* Peered cautiously round the corner
* *Closed up behind him*
* Kept contact with him by a hand on his shoulder
* *Quickened their pace*
* Crossed the road quickly
* Sprinted around the corner
* Scampered across the . . .
* Scurried off round the . . .
* Ran on, keeping their heads low
* Launched himself across the path
* *Walked confidently inside as if she belonged there*

SENTENCES

Tom made a stirrup with his hands, took her weight and hoisted her up to the top of the wall.

She straddled the wall with ease, swinging her trailing leg over swiftly and landing on the other side nimbly and without a sound.

Senses fully alert, they advanced, hunched over in a crouch and vaulted over the fence.

Writhing and twisting, Katie crawled through the gap and emerged into a low, dark cave.

They crept cautiously through the reeds to scan the area with their night-vision goggles.

Hugging the wall with her back, she shuffled sideways, one foot crossing the other.

As he inched forward, Tom felt along the wall for any holes in the rock.

All he could do was move as quickly and quietly as possible and hope he wasn't seen.

Tom waited for a moment and then followed. He peeped around the corner of the building. There was no one there.

Staying close to the walls, Tom edged round the compound, paused . . . nothing stirred, moved closer to the building, paused again to listen for any unnatural sounds, then sprinted across the yard, and dived behind a lorry for cover.

Pressing himself against the wall, he made his way towards the main entrance.

Katie skirted the rear of the buildings, hugging the shadows, peering furtively around corners and halting at every rustle.

Quickly rolling onto her side, Katie strained her neck upwards to peer through the window.

He came to the corner and cautiously peered around it, not knowing what he was going to find on the other side.

Katie sprinted around the corner, hoping that she would make it across the yard without being seen.

Keeping low, Tom scampered across the park to the nearest hedge.

Katie knew if she wasn't going to be stopped, she had to walk inside confidently as if she belonged there.

D. Getting inside

WORDS	

Nouns	**Entrance**, exit, way out
	Gate, door, grille, walls, window, shutters
	Bolts, bars, lock, padlock, handle, chain, keypad
	Guards, sentries
Adjectives	**Wooden**, metal, glass
	Thick, wide, heavy, high, massive
	Small, narrow
	Odd, misshapen
	Old, ancient, rotting
Verbs	**Secured**, locked, fastened
	Found, located

Pushed, pulled, tugged, yanked, thrust, plucked, kicked, slammed, jammed

Eased, opened, lifted, turned, swung, slid, rolled

Checked, tested, unlocked

Knocked, hammered

Entered, followed, crossed, stepped, walked, moved, edged, inched, slipped, crept, crawled, ducked, dived, flattened

Stood, waited, paused, hovered, leaned

Looked, peeped, peered, craned

Heard, clicked, hissed, swished, squeaked, rattled, thumped

PHRASES – NOUNS AND ADJECTIVES

- ★ Only one door
- ★ No other way out
- ★ *As quietly as he could, he . . .*
- ★ Like a panther
- ★ *Ancient handle*
- ★ Glass door
- ★ Steel door
- ★ Thick metal door
- ★ *Two heavy bolts at the top and bottom*
- ★ Thick iron bar
- ★ Huge padlock on the door
- ★ *One small window – old, wooden and rotting*
- ★ Illuminated numerical keypad
- ★ *Sound of bolts and bars*
- ★ Rattle of a chain on the other side
- ★ *Pitch black beyond*
- ★ Flickering light in the darkness

PHRASES – VERBS

- ★ Waited for an answering flash from the trees
- ★ Checked that no one was watching
- ★ Had not been followed
- ★ *Moved slowly across the hall*
- ★ Inched his way to the corner of the landing
- ★ Edged closer to the door, one on each side
- ★ Hovered outside the door
- ★ *Shifted the metal racks*

* Revealed an ancient-looking door set in the wall
* Rolled the dial
* *Turned and walked up to a wooden door*
* Leaned closer and put his ear to the door
* Put his eye to the crack
* Put her eye to the narrow gap between the hinges
* Craned their necks to see what was inside
* *Stood poised at the handle*
* Turned the knob
* Tugged on the handle
* Yanked on the handle
* Tested the locked door
* Eased down the handle, a fraction at a time
* Took hold of the handle, paused, turned it swiftly and entered
* Scrabbled at the front door
* Reached out towards the door, hand shaking
* *Gave the door a cautious push*
* Eased the door open a crack
* Eased the door ajar
* Let the door drift open slowly
* Opened the door a couple of centimetres . . . opened it a bit more
* Put his shoulder to the door and pushed
* Took a step forward
* Launched a massive kick at the door
* Kicked the door open
* Threw his weight against the door and plunged inside
* *Stepped through the door*
* Slipped through the door into the darkness
* Catapulted through the door
* Moved fast and dashed inside
* Entered the room at speed
* Ducked sideways
* *As instructed . . .*
* Knocked on the door three times
* Waited, knocked three times more
* Uttered a password to the sentry
* Stepped aside and allowed them to enter
* Hammered on it urgently
* *Heard the rattle of a chain*
* Drawn on the other side
* Clicked from the inside
* Hissed open
* Heard the noise of bolts being drawn back
* Clicked loudly as it unlocked and opened

☆ Rattled as some invisible bolt was released
☆ *Squeaked upward*
☆ Swished open
☆ Started to swing inwards
☆ Slid shut
☆ *Secured with padlocks*
☆ Fastened with a thick iron bar across the door
☆ Took note of the huge padlock on the door
☆ *Put his foot on the first rung*
☆ Took his weight
☆ Climbed the ladder until he was level with the window
☆ *Eased open a wooden shutter*
☆ Peered gingerly through . . .
☆ Pushed the sash window upwards
☆ Slid his penknife into the gap and eased the window open
☆ *Climbed inside*
☆ Climbed through the gap
☆ Slid the window shut behind him
☆ *Began to creep along the roof tiles*
☆ Flattened his body against the slates
☆ *Thrust his hand out in front of him*
☆ Edged their way carefully
☆ Used their outstretched hands to guide them
☆ Ran it along the wall until he located the light switch
☆ *Jammed a piece of paper in the hinge*
☆ Prevented the door closing fully

SENTENCES

He yanked on the handle. It wouldn't budge. It was locked.

He turned the handle and gave the door a cautious push. He waited a few minutes before going inside.

Leaning closer, Katie put her ear to the door. Nothing. She tugged on the handle, and slipped through the door.

She eased down the handle, a fraction at a time; stopped a moment and listened. The rusty hinges hadn't squeaked. She opened it a bit more, unsure of what she would discover inside.

He thrust his hand out in front of him, and ran it along the wall until he located the light switch.

A lock clicked from the inside, followed by the rattle of a chain and a bolt being drawn back.

There was a buzz and the metal gates swished open and a large, black car with tinted windows emerged. The gates slid quickly shut again. There was not enough time for him to slip through before they slid closed.

No one had followed her. She turned quickly, headed for the house with the black, wooden door and hammered on it urgently.

As instructed, he knocked three times, waited three seconds and knocked three times more.

She slid her penknife into the gap and eased the window open.

She climbed inside and carefully slid the window shut behind her.

Katie pushed the sash window upwards, climbed through the gap and landed in a crouch.

Creeping along the roof tiles, his body flat to the roof, Tom gripped the tiles, felt for ridges with his feet and edged slowly towards the open window.

He put his foot on the first rung of the rickety, wooden ladder. It held his weight. Carefully, he tested the next rung. It creaked but didn't break. Rung by rung, he ascended the ladder, testing each one as he went until he was level with the balcony. Heaving himself over the rail, he inched his way to the sliding doors.

Tom jammed a piece of paper into the hinge to stop the door closing fully.

SECTION 3 – REACTION

WORDS

Nouns	**Panic**, urge
	Swallow, breath, gasp, murmur, whisper
	Neck, back, tingle, prickle
	Hands, palms, sweat
Adjectives	**Cautious**, nervous, anxious, alert
	Tingling, prickling, spider-like
	Cold, ice-cold, hollow, tight
Verbs	**Tensed**, warned, urged
	Ran, crawled, leaped, churned, pounded
	Swallowed, smothered, clamped
	Looked, glanced, checked, strained, watched
	Sank, lowered, trailed off, whispered

Shivered, shuddered

Forced, willed, fought, mustered

Shrank back

Ran, fled

Adverbs   **Quickly**, cautiously, furtively, nervously

PHRASES – NOUNS AND ADJECTIVES

★ Every muscle in his body
★ Every nerve in her body
★ Tingling sensation
★ A tingling sixth sense
★ Distinct feeling
★ Nervous swallow
★ *A slow chill*
★ A cold, spider-like sensation
★ Ice-cold shiver
★ *Surge of adrenalin*
★ A trickle of sweat
★ *Hollow feeling*
★ Tight knot in the pit of her stomach
★ *Like a startled owl*

PHRASES – VERBS

★ Something was very wrong
★ Alert to any danger
★ Warned him he was walking into trouble
★ Had the distinct feeling he was being watched
★ Felt as if there were eyes everywhere
★ *Tensed and shrank back into the shadows as . . .*
★ Tensed his body and urged himself to jump
★ Willed himself to move and soon . . .
★ Fought back the urge to flee
★ Mustered up the courage and . . .
★ *Shot through her*
★ Crawled down his spine
★ *Broke out on his upper lip*
★ Broke out on her palms
★ Rubbed them dry on her trousers
★ *Heart pounded*

- ⋆ Leaped in her chest like a wild salmon
- ⋆ *Held her breath*
- ⋆ Let out a shallow gasp
- ⋆ Forced herself to breathe slowly
- ⋆ *Made him look sharply backwards*
- ⋆ Looked nervously round every corner
- ⋆ Checked nervously over her shoulder
- ⋆ Glanced round nervously as he heard . . .
- ⋆ Flickered from side to side
- ⋆ Strained for the sound of footsteps
- ⋆ *Flickered across her face*
- ⋆ Betrayed her nervousness
- ⋆ *Lowered her voice*
- ⋆ Sank to a murmur
- ⋆ (voice) trailed off as she realised what lay ahead
- ⋆ Covered her mouth and whispered through her fingers

SENTENCES

Something was very wrong. He could feel it. A tingling sixth sense of danger lurking in the shadows.

Every muscle in her body tensed. She was constantly alert for the sound of footsteps.

A cold, spider-like sensation crawled down her spine. The prickling sensation moved to her fingers. She felt a cold sweat break out above her upper lip.

As a surge of adrenalin shot through her, every nerve in Katie's body was on high alert.

Tom had the distinct feeling they were being watched from one of the upper windows. Sweat broke out on the palms of his hands and he had to keep rubbing them dry on his trousers.

A tight knot in the pit of her stomach warned Gail she was walking into trouble. Shuddering, she fought back the urge to flee.

He glanced round nervously as he heard the snap of a twig behind him. His eyes flickered from side to side and he lowered his voice.

His voice trailed off as he realised what lay ahead.

The skin on the back of his neck prickled as he approached the entrance. The place felt evil. It was the type of place that made people quicken their step as they passed.

Cautiously, she reached out towards the door, her hand shaking and adrenalin surging through her veins.

5

Secret passages and tunnels

He tapped, pushed, pulled at bits of the heavy carved panelling near the fireplace. Eventually, one of the wooden leaves turned in his hand. **His eyes widened and he gasped.** A section of the wooden panel had clicked open like a flap to reveal a hidden passage – a low, dark tunnel leading deep underground.

Where water had leaked in from the rocks, the walls and floor glistened with damp. They edged down the glistening, stone stairs – slipping and sliding on the moss-covered steps. A **piercing scream echoed** around the tunnel as her foot skidded from under her. She made a grab for Tom's arm. But she was too late.

Suddenly, millions of bats, like a black plume of smoke, fluttered from every corner. **Her eyes wide with terror**, she flapped her hands madly in front of her. The passage rang with the **echoes of her shrieking**.

His heart hammered in his chest as the torch flickered and died, and he was left floundering around in the dark, feeling his way with his outstretched hands against the tunnel walls.

SECTION 1 – SECRET PASSAGES

Setting

Nouns	**Tunnels**, labyrinth, maze
	Hall, passage, room, study, lounge

Basement, cellar, vault

Door, floor, wall, panel, panelling, fireplace, mantelpiece

Corner, section

Trapdoor, manhole cover, opening, board

Handle, ring, chain, hinge

Flight, stairs, stairway, steps

Darkness, shadows, candles, candle-holders, torchlight, torches

Noise, whisper

Touch, cobwebs, mould, dust

Glow, gleam

Air, breeze, waft, smell, stench, reek

Adjectives

Narrow, tiny, wide, large, steep, spiral, endless

Wooden, stone, metal, iron, brass, silver

Hidden, secret, gaping, sliding, shut

Triangular, round, door-shaped, odd, misshapen

Rusting, rickety

Clammy, stale, cold, icy, freezing

Black, red, flaming, inky, blank

Billowing, flickering, dying, dim

Verbs

Concealed, disguised

Built, fitted, poked, jutted

Moved, appeared, rose, dropped, opened

Vanished, disappeared

Turned, swung, revolved, pivoted

Revealed, glimpsed, filtered, filled

Carved, hewn

Felt, prickled, brushed

Heard, clicked, creaked

PHRASES – NOUNS AND ADJECTIVES

★ Just below his eye-line
★ *A secret bolt-hole*
★ Priest hole
★ *Extra door in the lounge*
★ Rickety door in the furthest corner
★ In the upper part of the door
★ *A tiny section of the wooden panel*
★ Heavy carved panelling near the fireplace
★ *When it was shut, the stone was . . .*
★ Blank wall
★ A mass of stone
★ Block of stone on a hinge
★ A triangular block of stone
★ The section of the wall to the right of the fireplace
★ Door-shaped opening in the corner of the room
★ *Ring of black iron*
★ Iron ring handle of the studded door
★ Chain dangling in the corner
★ Creaking rope on its rusty hinges
★ *A sliding trapdoor*
★ A large round board like a wooden manhole cover
★ *Until at last it . . .*
★ Very slowly, the great stone . . .
★ *A large opening in the wall*
★ Opening wide enough to . . .
★ Gaping hole in the woodblock floor
★ *Secret door*
★ Metal doors
★ Vault door
★ Wooden trap door
★ Dark hole
★ *Narrow flight of steps*
★ A small metal rung
★ Hidden staircase
★ Little stairway
★ Set of narrow stone stairs
★ Flight of rickety wooden steps
★ Steep, narrow flight of stairs
★ Steep natural stairway
★ Flight of spiral steps
★ Endless flight of crumbling moss-covered steps
★ *Carpet of dust*
★ A current of cold air

PHRASES – VERBS

- ★ *Concealed behind the tapestry*
- ★ Disguised as a bookcase
- ★ Appeared solid and unbroken
- ★ Built into a huge stone pillar
- ★ Built into the floor
- ★ Poked out of the floor
- ★ Sunk into the boards
- ★ Set inside the buttress
- ★ Fitted so that it was impossible to find it inside the room
- ★ Glimpsed the edge of a curved slab of wood
- ★ Moved by a lever and a rope
- ★ *Swung aside to reveal*
- ★ Pivoted ponderously
- ★ Pivoted on a central axis
- ★ Began to slide backwards
- ★ Clicked open like a flap
- ★ Rose slowly from the floor
- ★ Slid up into the stonework
- ★ Creaked up out of the stone
- ★ Rose until it vanished altogether
- ★ Vanished into the rock above
- ★ Clicked open a door
- ★ Opened to unsuspecting intruders
- ★ *Revealed a trap door*
- ★ Must lead somewhere
- ★ Lead down to . . .
- ★ Opened into . . .
- ★ Widened into another room
- ★ Went off in all directions
- ★ Dropped deeper underground
- ★ Led down into a black void
- ★ Led down at a steep angle
- ★ Disappeared inside the cliff
- ★ Twisted steeply to the tunnel below
- ★ Corkscrewed up through the building
- ★ Stretched unseen into the unfathomable darkness
- ★ *Grew accustomed to the light*
- ★ Could just make out . . .
- ★ Caught a glimpse of . . .
- ★ Disappeared out of sight
- ★ Grew darker
- ★ Peered into the inky blackness

- ★ Made it appear that the shadows were reaching out to him
- ★ Drove out the light
- ★ *Prickled his bare arms*
- ★ Brushed her back
- ★ Swung closed behind them
- ★ *Had set foot in there for centuries*
- ★ Saw . . . carved into the passage wall
- ★ *Heard a whisper of sound*
- ★ Could hear footsteps ringing out
- ★ Filtered through the grille in the wall
- ★ Hewn from the stone

SENTENCES

A section of the wooden panel clicked open like a flap to reveal a hidden passage.

A large opening in the wall revealed a set of stairs that twisted steeply to the tunnel below.

Tom noticed that one of the stones jutted out more than the others. As he pressed the stone, a section of the wall to his right moved, sending a current of cold air brushing against his bare arms.

Suddenly, she heard the muffled sound of a locking mechanism releasing within the stonework. Then, part of the wall pivoted and swung aside to reveal a spiral flight of stairs.

Gail noticed a rickety door in the furthest corner, hidden in the shadows. When she got close to the door, she noticed that it was studded with black nails, and one of the panels was carved with ancient symbols.

Poking out of the floor was a rusting iron ring. A trapdoor had been built into the floor.

Interaction

WORDS

Nouns   **Panel**, panelling, fireplace, mantelpiece, door

                      Trapdoor, stones, stonework

                      Ring, chain, hinge, disc, wooden leaves, locking mechanism

                      Head, hand, palm

                      Flight, stairs, stairway, steps

Adjectives	**Hidden**, secret
	Iron, stone
	Small, round
	Crumbling, moss-covered
	Carved
Verbs	**Felt**, thrust, pressed, grasped, pushed, pulled, tugged, heaved
	Twisted, turned, tapped, slid
	Stood, descended
	Peered, gazed
	Released, swung, revolved

PHRASES – NOUNS AND ADJECTIVES

* ★ Huge fireplace
* ★ Handle of a hidden door
* ★ Rusting iron ring
* ★ Block of stone on a hinge
* ★ Bits of the heavy carved panelling near the fireplace
* ★ One of the wooden leaves
* ★ Small, round disc
* ★ Crumbling, moss-covered steps

PHRASES – VERBS

* ★ Thrust her head into . . .
* ★ Felt around the inside
* ★ Felt around for a door
* ★ Grasped a chain dangling in the furthest corner
* ★ *Tugged the chain*
* ★ Tapped, pushed at . . .
* ★ Pressed the mantelpiece
* ★ Pushed it hard with his palm
* ★ Twisted it anti-clockwise
* ★ Pushed at the central panel
* ★ Pushed aside a pile of stones
* ★ *Turned in his hand*
* ★ Released a locking mechanism in the stonework
* ★ Slid back
* ★ Heaved back the . . .

* Swung the door open
* *Stood on the top step*
* Tumbled through the opening
* Disappeared in the blink of an eye
* Revolved again and he was back in the room
* Pulled the trapdoor behind them
* Descended an endless flight of . . .

SENTENCES

Tapping and pushing at bits of the heavy carved panelling near the fireplace, he eventually found one of the wooden leaves that turned in his hand.

He felt around the block of stone until he found a small, round disc.

He removed the top stones from the cairn, and then moved the rest aside until he glimpsed the edge of a curved slab of wood.

He tugged at the wooden cover and revealed a hidden staircase that corkscrewed underground.

Thrusting her head into the great fireplace, Katie felt around the inside. Her hand suddenly grasped a chain dangling in the furthest corner.

When she tugged on the chain, a section of the wooden panelling to the side of the fireplace slid open like a door, revealing a set of narrow stone stairs that corkscrewed up through the building.

Quickly, he descended an endless flight of crumbling, moss-covered steps.

SECTION 2 – TUNNELS

Setting

WORDS

Nouns	**Maze**, labyrinth, crypt, vault
	Passages, passageways, path, stairs, walls, niches
	Light, lamp, torch, beam
	Stone, rock
	Stench, dust, water, bats, skulls
Adjectives	**Long**, low, narrow, twisting, steep
	Huge, small

Dark, black, inky, gloomy, dim, shadowy, ghostly, eerie, green, red

Slippery, dangerous

Security, emergency

Cold, damp, glistening

Putrid, sickly

Rough, smooth

Gushing, crashing

Burning

Verbs   **Bent**, curved, wound, twisted, turned, coiled, snaked

Led, stretched, opened, enclosed, branched

Sloped, climbed, ascended, dropped, descended

Squeezed, crawled

Lit, illuminated, pierced

Revealed, glimpsed

Heard, boomed, crackled, crunched, dripped, echoed

Sculpted, carved

Polished, glistened

Startled, disturbed, flew, fluttered

Burned, sputtered, flickered

PHRASES – NOUNS AND ADJECTIVES

* Low, dark tunnels
* Long, twisting path
* Narrow tunnel
* Labyrinth with an endless puzzle of staircases and tunnels
* Inky black maze of dangerous, slippery paths
* Labyrinthine set of passageways and niches
* Barely enough headroom
* *Niches in the walls*
* A hole in the rock the size of a small door
* *Clammy, cold, icy to the touch*
* As cold as a crypt
* Cold air all around them. Icy cold
* Like a cold, dry mouth

- ★ *Light of one dim candle*
- ★ Silver gleam
- ★ Brass candleholders on the wall
- ★ Odd, misshapen shadows
- ★ Inky blackness
- ★ Tinted red by the flaming torchlight
- ★ Billowing torches
- ★ Flickering light of a flaming torch
- ★ A dim glow
- ★ Torch in the niche
- ★ Burning torches
- ★ Ghostly light
- ★ Beam of the torch
- ★ Beam of light
- ★ White light
- ★ A huge shadow
- ★ Dark space between each dim lamp
- ★ *Somewhere in the distance*
- ★ Rattling noise like a chain being dropped into a coffin
- ★ Dying echo in the freezing passage
- ★ Humming sound
- ★ Crashing wave
- ★ Dripping water
- ★ Gushing water
- ★ *Putrid, sickly stench*
- ★ Waft of stale air
- ★ Cobwebs and mould

PHRASES – VERBS

- ★ *Wound underground*
- ★ Twisted and turned like a maze
- ★ Began to bend to the right
- ★ Curved so far she could no longer see the opening
- ★ Dropped off at a sharp angle
- ★ Stretched back deep into the cliff
- ★ Led off in different directions
- ★ Branched into several tunnels
- ★ Opened out into an underground chamber
- ★ Sloped downhill
- ★ *Pointed the beam of the torch ahead*
- ★ Marked flickering pathways
- ★ Crackled down the passage like a camera flash
- ★ Had a dim light to guide his steps

- ★ Pierced the shadows
- ★ Lit only by the narrow beam of light from the torch
- ★ Lit at long intervals
- ★ Lit by the green glow of an emergency light
- ★ Illuminated a steep, natural stairway
- ★ *Glimpsed a shelf of grinning skulls*
- ★ Revealed glimpses of . . .
- ★ Covered in pictures of . . .
- ★ Carved into the rock
- ★ Glistened with damp
- ★ *Heard echoes*
- ★ Filled the tunnel
- ★ Crunched on the broken shells and bones
- ★ Echoed and crashed back at him
- ★ Heard a shout echoing through the caves
- ★ Rang with the echoes of his scream
- ★ Dripped from the ceiling and echoed around the walls
- ★ Boomed like a clap of thunder
- ★ Burned down and sputtered
- ★ *Felt cold under his hands*
- ★ Struck the wall beneath her and sprayed upwards
- ★ Polished into dangerous, slippery paths
- ★ Sculpted into jagged blades
- ★ *Disturbed a number of squadrons of bats*
- ★ Came towards them, flying in close formation
- ★ Fluttered from every corner
- ★ Flew out through . . .

SENTENCES

The cave was a winding, underground maze of low, dark tunnels.

Where water had leaked in from the rocks, the walls and floor glistened with damp.

It began to bend to the right and soon it had curved so far that looking back they could no longer see the opening.

As they climbed down the steep, stone stairway, a blast of cold air crashed into them. The tunnel was as cold as a crypt and dark as night.

The air was cold all around him. Icy cold. As he continued down, a waft of stale air drifted towards him. In the flickering light it looked like the odd, misshapen shadows were reaching out to him. The corridor grew darker, the air got staler. Peering into the inky blackness, he caught a glimpse of movement.

Interaction

WORDS

Nouns	**Cavern**, opening, hole, slope, path, walls, niches
	Bats, skulls
	Light, lamp, torch, beam
	Smoke, plume
	Echoes
Adjectives	**Long**, narrow, twisting, steep, precipitous
	Damp, dangerous
	Black, smoky, sputtering
Verbs	**Ventured**, emerged, followed, crossed
	Squeezed, edged, descended
	Slipped, slid, skidded
	Glimpsed, fluttered, flapped
	Rang, echoed

PHRASES – NOUNS AND ADJECTIVES

- ★ A huge cavern
- ★ Steep slope
- ★ Precipitous path
- ★ Damp and dangerous
- ★ Niches in the walls
- ★ Millions of bats, like a black plume of smoke

PHRASES – VERBS

- ★ Ventured further in
- ★ Squeezed through the hole
- ★ Edged down the . . .
- ★ *Emerged into an opening*
- ★ Led off in all different directions
- ★ Followed the long, twisting path
- ★ Descended a precipitous path

- ★ Moved through the tunnel
- ★ Crossed a narrow ledge
- ★ Edged down the stone steps
- ★ Squeezed along a murky corridor
- ★ Pulled her deeper into the blackness
- ★ Squeezed through a hole
- ★ Descended a precipitous path into a huge cavern
- ★ Emerged from the passage into . . .
- ★ *Used the light from their torch to guide their steps*
- ★ Followed the smoky light of the sputtering torch
- ★ Glimpsed a shelf of grinning skulls
- ★ Stopped to search . . .
- ★ *Fluttered from every corner*
- ★ Flapped his hands in front of him
- ★ Rang with the echoes of his scream
- ★ *Dripped from the roof*
- ★ Carved out of the rocky wall

SENTENCES

They followed the long, twisting path using the light from their torch to guide their steps.

Squeezing through the hole that had been carved out of the rocky wall, they descended a precipitous path into a huge cavern.

Following the smoky light of the sputtering torch, they moved cautiously through the tunnel, stopping to search the niches in the walls. Suddenly, to their left, they glimpsed a shelf of grinning skulls.

They edged down the glistening, stone steps – slipping and sliding on the damp steps. She grabbed his arm to steady herself as her foot skidded from under her.

Suddenly, millions of bats, like a black plume of smoke, fluttered from every corner and the passage rang with the echoes of his scream as he flapped his hands in front of him.

He ducked as a swish of wings rushed through the air and bats brushed his head with their furry bodies.

SECTION 3 – REACTION (SECRET PASSAGES AND TUNNELS)

WORDS

Nouns	**Brain**, heart, throat, chest, breath, neck, hands
	Instinct, sensation, panic
	Sound, footsteps, scream
Adjectives	**Dry**, ice-cold, tingling, lingering
	Fast, feverish
	Outstretched
	Echoing
Verbs	**Knew**, realised, remembered
	Stopped, tensed, fought
	Banged, clenched, squeezed
	Moved, edged, slithered
	Glanced, flickered
	Swallowed, gulped, gasped, screamed
	Felt, groped, floundered

PHRASES – NOUNS AND ADJECTIVES

★ Ice-cold needles into the back of his neck
★ Throat suddenly dry
★ Painful gasps
★ With his outstretched hands against the tunnel walls
★ Way out of the maze of tunnels
★ Echoing footsteps

PHRASES – VERBS

★ Had a tingling sensation that he wasn't alone
★ Tensed, fighting her body's natural instinct to run
★ Knew he had to think of something fast
★ Had to fight hard to . . .
★ Had a lingering chill

- ✳ Tried desperately to remember the way they had come
- ✳ Getting closer by the minute
- ✳ *Heart almost stopped*
- ✳ Clenched in panic
- ✳ Banged against his ribs
- ✳ Swallowed, his throat suddenly dry
- ✳ Coated her forehead
- ✳ *Glanced behind him*
- ✳ Glanced back over her shoulder
- ✳ *Felt his way*
- ✳ Floundered around in the dark
- ✳ *Slithered to a halt*

SENTENCES

She tensed, fighting her body's natural instinct to run, and she was having to fight hard to do so.

He had a lingering chill, as if someone was pushing ice-cold needles into the back of his neck.

His stomach clenched in panic and he knew he had to think of something fast. The sound of echoing footsteps was getting closer by the minute.

His heart banging against his ribs, he squeezed through the hole and swung the trapdoor shut behind him.

He swallowed, his throat suddenly dry.

He slithered to a halt, his breath coming in painful gasps.

As the torch flickered and died, he was left floundering around in the dark, feeling his way with his outstretched hands against the tunnel walls.

Her mind was working with feverish haste as she tried desperately to remember the way out of the maze of tunnels.

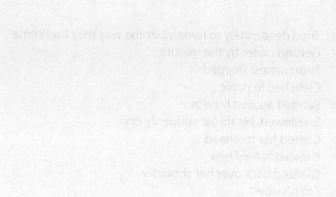

Part 2
The chase

6

Followed

Kitty couldn't shake off the strange sensation that she was being followed. All her senses were on high alert as she strained for the sound of footsteps.

A sudden movement across the street caught her attention . . . a flickering shadow in the gloom.

She glanced over. No one there.

She stopped dead in her tracks as she heard the sound of footsteps behind her. Kneeling down and pretending to tie her shoelaces, Kitty **dared another glance over her shoulder.**

SECTION 1 – CHARACTERS

WORDS	
Nouns	**Figure**, shadow, man, woman, face
	Movement, footsteps, sound, noise, whisper
Adjectives	**Still**, low, half-hidden, furtive
	Black, shadowy, visible
	Quiet, silent, sudden
Verbs	**Loomed**, silhouetted, appeared, emerged, parked
	Stood, moved, exposed
	Gone, vanished, disappeared
	Tracked, trailed
	Saw, glanced, looked, stared, watched, locked, recognised
	Heard, detected

PHRASES – NOUNS AND ADJECTIVES

* ★ A shadow in the night
* ★ Shadowy, hooded figure
* ★ Two furtive figures
* ★ Same woman
* ★ *Sudden movement*
* ★ Movement near the door
* ★ *No one there*
* ★ Nothing out of the ordinary
* ★ *Like a bloodhound following a scent*

PHRASES – VERBS

* ★ Stood perfectly still
* ★ Masked in the shadows
* ★ Silhouetted in the stairwell
* ★ *Appeared at one of the windows*
* ★ Reflected in the window
* ★ Half-hidden behind an ice-cream van
* ★ Could not see his face
* ★ Began to emerge
* ★ *Looking down on them*
* ★ Stared out across the courtyard
* ★ Stared directly at her
* ★ Glanced briefly in her direction
* ★ Locked eyes
* ★ Saw each other at the same moment
* ★ *Saw a movement ahead of her*
* ★ Detected a sudden movement
* ★ *Heard the noise again*
* ★ Heard footsteps behind her
* ★ Heard a low whisper
* ★ *Parked across the street*
* ★ Watched the front door
* ★ Vanished into the crowd
* ★ Tracking him for days
* ★ *Twitched as they passed*
* ★ Poked out like a sniper's gun

SENTENCES

She saw a movement near the door. A shadowy figure.

They had followed her from the library and were now parked across the street and watching the front door.

Two furtive figures had been tracking them for days like bloodhounds following a scent.

It was the same woman he had seen outside the café. He glanced briefly in her direction again, but she had vanished into the crowd.

A sudden movement . . . something glinting in the sun . . . behind the hedge. As he looked again, he spotted a camera lens poking out of the hedge like a sniper's gun.

A sudden movement across the street caught his attention . . . a flickering shadow in the gloom. He glanced over. No one there.

He looked up from his drink and they locked eyes. She had recognised him.

SECTION 2 – INTERACTION

WORDS

Nouns	**Pace**, steps, tracks
	Feet, shoulder, shoelace
	House, shop, street
	Glimpse
Adjectives	**Still**, motionless, frozen
	Cautious
Verbs	**Looked**, glanced, stole, scanned, searched
	Tensed, stiffened
	Backed, dived, rolled
	Dashed, rushed, raced
	Turned, spun, whirled, whipped round, sprang
	Manoeuvred, knelt, crouched
	Changed, varied, retraced, re-emerged

PHRASES – NOUNS AND ADJECTIVES

* ★ A quarter of a mile further on
* ★ Top of the alley
* ★ End of the passage

PHRASES – VERBS

* ★ Sat motionless for several minutes
* ★ Varied her pace
* ★ Hadn't gone very far
* ★ Changed direction
* ★ Kept ahead of her
* ★ *Looked round*
* ★ Looked again
* ★ Glanced over his shoulder
* ★ Glanced round furtively
* ★ Glanced up from his drink
* ★ Scanned the street
* ★ Kept looking over his shoulder
* ★ Raised his eyes to the house opposite
* ★ Stole another look over his shoulder
* ★ Tried to catch a glimpse of her watcher
* ★ *Sprang to his feet*
* ★ Spun round
* ★ Backed into the . . .
* ★ Whipped round
* ★ Turned round suddenly
* ★ Turned and retraced his steps
* ★ Dived into a shop
* ★ Re-emerged further down the street
* ★ Dashed to the spot
* ★ *Stopped dead in his tracks*
* ★ Knelt and pretended to be tying his shoelace
* ★ Manoeuvred around her bedroom

SENTENCES

He stopped dead in his tracks as he heard the sound of footsteps behind him. Quickly, he changed direction, raced down an alley, and ducked behind a wheelie bin.

He kept glancing behind him, every muscle in his body tensed, and quickened his pace.

She looked round furtively, covered her mouth and whispered through her fingers.

Kneeling down and pretending to tie his shoelaces, Rob dared to glance over his shoulder.

She sat motionless for several minutes whilst she scanned the café. Then Kitty sprang up and darted to the door.

Crouching on all fours, Kitty manoeuvred around her bedroom towards the window. Slowly, she lifted her head above the sill and peered out from behind the curtain.

SECTION 3 – REACTION

WORDS

Nouns	**Feeling**, sensation, instinct
	Something, presence
	Eyes, sight, voice, sound, whisper, murmur
	Muscles, nerves
Adjectives	**Curious**, sinister, uncomfortable
Verbs	**Felt**, sensed, thought, hoped
	Knew, convinced, realised
	Could not, dared not
	Spotted, strained, flickered
	Tracked, trailed

PHRASES – NOUNS AND ADJECTIVES

* ⭐ Something behind him
* ⭐ Directly at him
* ⭐ *An uneasy feeling*
* ⭐ Gut instinct
* ⭐ Curious sensation
* ⭐ An uncomfortable feeling
* ⭐ A cold spider-like sensation
* ⭐ Every muscle in his body
* ⭐ Every nerve in her body

PHRASES – VERBS

* ☆ Couldn't shake the sinister sensation
* ☆ Sensed something behind him
* ☆ Felt a presence behind him
* ☆ *Crawl down his spine*
* ☆ Go up on the back of her neck
* ☆ Felt as if there were eyes everywhere
* ☆ Convinced himself he was imagining things
* ☆ *Thought he caught sight of . . .*
* ☆ Spotted her
* ☆ Recognized him
* ☆ Could feel her eyes
* ☆ Burning into his back
* ☆ Tracking their every move
* ☆ (eyes) flickered left and right
* ☆ Realised that the entrance was being watched
* ☆ *Dared not turn round*
* ☆ Dared not acknowledge
* ☆ *Sank to a murmur*
* ☆ Strained for the sound of . . .
* ☆ (voice) trailed off as he spotted . . .
* ☆ Covered her mouth
* ☆ Whispered through her fingers
* ☆ *Knew he had to shake her off*

SENTENCES

She sensed someone behind her and felt the hairs go up on the back of her neck.

Her voice sank to a murmur as she realized that the entrance was being watched.

Rubbing his sweating brow with his forearm, Rob's eyes flickered nervously left and right.

His voice trailed off as he spotted the same woman again.

Kitty couldn't shake off the strange sensation that she was being followed. All her senses were on high alert as she strained for the sound of footsteps.

Robert felt a cold, spider-like sensation crawl down his back. He felt as if there were eyes everywhere, following his every move.

7
Hiding

1. As the sound of footsteps drew closer, **a shiver charged down her spine like an electric shock**. She ducked back into one of the smaller rooms and stood there, behind the door.
2. They stopped outside the room. He could hear them talking into their phones. As the door slammed open, **every nerve in his body warned him not to move**, even though his arm was **shaking, and pins and needles prickled painfully in his ankle**.
3. The two sentries stopped metres from where she was crouched in the reeds. They scanned the area, looking for a trail. Lowering herself to the ground inside the ditch, Kitty was **shaking with terror and dread** that at any moment they would glance in her direction and she would be discovered.

    A squelch of feet in the mud broke the silence. They were moving away from her hiding place. She **held her breath**, waited a few minutes longer, and then peered over the muddy lip.

SECTION 1 – CHARACTERS

WORDS

Nouns	**Pursuers**, assailants, opponents, enemy
	Guards, sentries
	Presence, shadows, movement
	Sounds, feet, footsteps, boots
	Voices, whispers, murmurs, shouts, screams
	Squelch, rattle, creak, snap

Twig, branch, stone, gravel, mud

Lock, door, floorboard

Adjectives   **Low**, urgent

            Close, near

Verbs   **Moved**, walked, headed, turned, reached

            Stopped, paused, waited

            Raced, passed

            Disappeared, vanished

            Searched, stared, scanned

            Opened, closed

PHRASES – NOUNS AND ADJECTIVES

- *Darkness of a blind alley*
- Barely noticeable in the shadows
- *Beneath their feet*
- Outside the room
- Close to where he lay in the shadows
- Any minute . . .
- Unaware of his presence
- Oblivious to his presence below them
- Not aware that he was hidden in the . . .
- *Squelch of their feet in the mud*
- Thud of boots
- Creak of a floorboard
- Snap of a twig nearby
- Rattle of a lock
- Low, urgent whispers

PHRASES – VERBS

- *Turned the corner, talking into their phones*
- Scanned the yard with their eyes
- Skulking in the shadows
- Stopped outside the room
- Disappeared round the corner
- Stopped at the edge of . . .
- *Drew closer*
- Passed within metres of where they were . . .

* Could hear their voices getting closer
* Going to be opened at any moment
* Could have reached out and touched him
* *Didn't look in his direction*
* Stared down for a brief second
* Hadn't seen him
* Passed directly overhead
* Walked straight past him
* Raced passed

SENTENCES

They were heading in his direction. He could hear the thud of their boots as they moved close to where he lay in the shadows.

They stopped outside the room. He could hear them talking into their phones. Any minute they would open the door. He had to find somewhere to hide . . . and quick.

They were unaware of his presence, skulking in the shadows behind them. They didn't look in his direction. If they had looked for more than a few seconds they would have seen him.

The two sentries stopped metres from where he was crouched in the reeds. They scanned the area, looking for a trail. He could hear the squelch of their feet in the mud.

She slipped further into the shadows and flattened herself against the wall.

SECTION 2 – INTERACTION

WORDS

Nouns	**Pursuers**, assailants, opponents, enemy
	Silence, darkness, shadows, candle, torch, light
	Head, face, hood, knees, haunches, back, stomach, belly, chest
	Mountain, rocks, boulders
	Woodland, treeline, trees, branches, trunk, logs, reeds, foliage, leaves, pine needles, shrub, bush, hedge, grass
	Floor, ground, ditch, trench, hole
	Roof, room, walls, door, window, stairs, steps, staircase, fire escape, banister, crowd

Couch, seats, chair, curtains, table, desk

Crates, boxes, chests, racks

Bars, grille, mesh

Road, vehicle, car, van

Sounds, feet, footsteps

Voices, whispers, murmurs, shouts, screams

Adjectives   **Metal**, steel, iron, stone, brick

Thick, wide, low, hanging

Dark, shadowy, enveloping

Automatic, instinctive

Verbs   **Dug**, scooped out, covered, hid, concealed

Heard, listened

Saw, watched, looked, glanced, peeped, peered, searched

Lay, sat, waited, poised, leaned, moved

Merged, submerged, vanished

Hugged, pressed, pinned, wedged, flattened

Lifted, raised, craned

Inched, edged, eased, slunk, crept, crawled, slithered, rolled

Slid, slipped, dipped, bowed, ducked, dropped, dived

Sank, lowered, shrank, sneaked, backed, retreated

Hit, threw, flung, jerked

Darted, scurried, scattered, scrambled, stumbled, staggered

PHRASES – NOUNS AND ADJECTIVES

★ Out of sight of anyone waiting
★ Still no sign of them
★ *With an automatic action*
★ With every step, he . . .
★ *Enveloping darkness*
★ Thick, dark woodland
★ *Trunk of the tree*
★ Nearest tree
★ Wide trunk
★ Hanging willow trees

- Pile of logs
- *Muddy lip of the ditch*
- A rocky crag
- *Low brick wall*
- Stone wall
- *Metal grille*
- Steel mesh
- *Approaching feet*
- Emergency stairs
- First flight of steps
- *Pile of boxes*

PHRASES – VERBS

- *Hid amongst . . .*
- Hid when she heard . . .
- Looked around for a place to hide
- Searched the room for a hiding place
- Backed away and set about finding somewhere to hide
- *Slipped into the shadows*
- Lay in the shadows under . . .
- Slunk back into the shadows
- Stuck to the shadows
- Shied away from the flickering street lamps
- Retreated into the shadow behind the . . .
- Had learned to move through the . . . in the dark
- Was able to blend into the shadows
- *Shrank back against the wall, glancing from side to side*
- Backed quietly away towards the . . .
- Staggered back
- Scurried for cover behind
- Stopped, spun around, and dropped onto his belly
- Turned, and melted back into the . . .
- Vanished in the crowd
- *Dipped his head*
- Dropped onto her knees
- Ducked and rolled underneath the . . .
- Ducked back into one of the smaller rooms and stood there
- Ducked down, seeking cover behind the . . .
- Dived backwards into the shadows
- Dived the last few feet into the shelter of the . . .
- *Lowered herself to the ground*
- Sank to her hands and knees

- ★ Dropped his back against the wall
- ★ Sank down at the base of one of the trees
- ★ Slid back against the . . . on to his haunches
- ★ Crouched down behind the . . . so he couldn't be seen
- ★ Crouched behind the rocks halfway up the slope
- ★ Crouched and peered through the . . .
- ★ *All dropped flat*
- ★ Went to ground
- ★ Hit the dirt
- ★ Flung herself down behind . . .
- ★ Scrambled for cover behind the . . .
- ★ Threw himself to the floor
- ★ Threw herself to the ground behind the . . .
- ★ Scattered, diving for cover
- ★ Darted behind the . . .
- ★ Stumbled among the rosebushes
- ★ *Had frozen in mid-crawl*
- ★ Poised on one knee and one muddy hand
- ★ *Dug herself in deeply behind a shrub*
- ★ Covered herself with leaves and pine needles
- ★ Climbed up the oak until she found a sturdy fork in the tree where she could stay undetected
- ★ Dragged herself into the tangled bushes at the base of the trees
- ★ Scooped out a hollow under the bushes
- ★ Was invisible from just a few metres away
- ★ *Waited in edgy silence*
- ★ Waited without moving
- ★ Hadn't moved a muscle for ten minutes
- ★ Waited a few minutes longer
- ★ Waited silently in the shadows until he was sure that . . .
- ★ Waited, motionless, for what seemed like an eternity
- ★ Watched as they hunted for him
- ★ Jerked her head back into the shadows
- ★ *Sat cross-legged on the floor in the shadows*
- ★ All he could do was lie there hugging the ground
- ★ Waited on the stairs, sitting down carefully and drawing her knees up against her chest so she couldn't be seen
- ★ *Crept along the floor against the wall until she was . . .*
- ★ Crawled underneath . . . so that she was hidden by . . .
- ★ Crawled to the edge of the bushes and peered out
- ★ Rolled to the ground, flattening himself against . . .
- ★ Rolled into the high grass so that she was out of sight
- ★ *Flattened himself against the . . .*
- ★ Wedged himself behind . . .

- ★ Pressed her back against the . . .
- ★ Pinned herself against a building
- ★ Eased himself up behind a . . .
- ★ *Covered his head with his hands*
- ★ Wrapped his arms round his head and ducked low
- ★ *Walked in the shadows of the road*
- ★ Kept off to the side in case a vehicle passed and spotted him
- ★ Kept his head down and face covered by the hood
- ★ Merged with the crowd and made his way out of the . . .
- ★ Bowed low so that his face would not be seen
- ★ *Peered over the . . .*
- ★ Sneaked a glance at . . .
- ★ Glanced up and peered through the steel mesh above her
- ★ Leaned forward so that she could see around the . . .
- ★ Peered through the posts of the banister
- ★ Edged carefully along until he was able to peer out
- ★ Peered back through the darkness
- ★ From where he was crouching he could see . . .
- ★ Leaned back out as far as he dared to . . .
- ★ Inched her head up to peer over the couch
- ★ See what his pursuers were doing without exposing his position
- ★ See if they were searching for them
- ★ *Listened for the sound of . . .*
- ★ Sat there listening intently
- ★ Heard voices coming up the stairs

SENTENCES

She ducked – and rolled underneath the van.

Tom flung himself down behind the tree.

He watched from underneath the bush as they hunted for him.

Lowering herself to the ground inside the ditch, she waited a few minutes longer, and then peered over the muddy lip.

She slipped further into the shadows and flattened herself against the wall.

Katie waited silently in the shadows until she was sure that the man wasn't coming back.

She waited on the stairs, sitting down carefully, drawing her knees up against her chest so she couldn't be seen.

She sat cross-legged on the floor in the shadows, and listened nervously for the sound of approaching feet.

He crawled underneath the first flight of steps so that he was hidden by the staircase.

He dived for cover and wedged himself behind a crate, and froze, motionless as if carved from stone.

As the sound of footsteps drew closer, she ducked back into one of the smaller rooms and stood there, behind the door, hardly daring to breathe.

Rob scooped out a hollow under the bushes and covered himself with leaves and pine needles.

She ducked down, seeking cover behind the reeds.

She peered through the posts of the banister, checking to see if they had gone.

She was crouched behind the willow tree. She hadn't moved a muscle for ten minutes. She waited – and still did not move. Still there was no sign of them. She peered through the hanging branches.

Cautiously, Kitty leaned forward so that she could see around the trunk of the tree.

He leaned back out as far as he dared to see what his pursuers were doing without exposing his position.

They all dropped flat, going to ground, and with an automatic action rolled into the high grass so that they were out of sight.

Keeping his head down and face covered by the hood so his face wouldn't show, he merged with the crowd and made his way out of the shopping centre.

SECTION 3 – REACTION

WORDS	
Nouns	**Fear**, dread, panic, terror, shock, horror
	Senses, sensation, nerves, brain, breathing, windpipe
	Danger, menace, darkness, shadow
	Thunder, squeak, snap
	Prayer
	Sound, voice, footsteps
	Body, spine, arm, ankle, chest, stomach
	Head, eyes, throat, temples, nose, lips
Adjectives	**Tingling**, electric, coiled, alert

Wide, still, frozen

Urgent, low, tight, choked

Verbs   **Gripped**, snaked, squeezed, choked

Surged, charged, pounded, hammered

Warned, dared, felt

Swallowed, stifled

Clasped, clenched, gritted

Looked, strained, blinked, glanced, peeped, peered, darted, closed

Shook, stood, waited, remained, froze, paralysed

PHRASES – NOUNS AND ADJECTIVES

* ⋆ At any moment . . .
* ⋆ *Every nerve in his body*
* ⋆ Tingling sixth sense
* ⋆ Like an electric shock
* ⋆ Sound of his own breathing
* ⋆ Like a coiled spring in the pit of her stomach
* ⋆ Wide eyes
* ⋆ *Certain they were somewhere nearby*
* ⋆ Hardly more than a whisper from the shadows
* ⋆ *Motionless, alert and ready to move quickly*
* ⋆ Motionless as if carved from stone

PHRASES – VERBS

* ⋆ *Surged through her*
* ⋆ Enveloped her
* ⋆ Brain quickened and all her senses were alert
* ⋆ Warned him not to make a sound
* ⋆ Until he passed
* ⋆ Wanted to get up and run
* ⋆ Knew she couldn't move
* ⋆ Didn't dare move as . . .
* ⋆ Tried to remain absolutely still
* ⋆ Only bit of him that was moving was his heart
* ⋆ Warned him not to move, even though . . .
* ⋆ Watched in horror as they moved closer to the stairs

* *Hammered in her chest as . . .*
* Was almost deafening in the silence
* Pounded in her temples
* Pounded so hard it seemed about to break his ribs
* *Held his breath*
* Hardly dared to breathe in case he was discovered
* Stifled a gasp
* Swallowed hard
* Kept his voice low
* Gripped him, snaking around his windpipe, choking his breath
* *Closed her eyes*
* Peeped round the . . .
* *Started to shake*
* Shaking with terror and dread that . . .
* Shook from the effort of holding herself still
* *Collected on his forehead*
* Trickled down the side of his nose into his eyes
* Panic flooded her face
* *Squeezed them shut and blinked rapidly*
* Strained to pierce the darkness
* Darted wildly from side to side
* *Clenched her teeth so hard her jaw ached*
* Moved her lips silently in prayer
* *Dropped to an urgent whisper*
* Whispered in a tight, choked voice
* Clasped her hands in her lap
* Prickled painfully in his ankle

SENTENCES

Every nerve in his body warned him not to move, even though his arm was shaking, and pins and needles prickled painfully in his ankle.

Kitty was shaking with terror and dread that at any moment they would glance in her direction and she would be discovered.

A tingling sixth sense made him look up. As he turned his head, he froze. They were standing right above him.

She wanted to get up and run, but she knew she couldn't. She had heard their boots thudding up the stairs.

Panic gripped him, snaking around his windpipe, choking his breath.

The sound of his own breathing was almost deafening in the silence.

As the blood pounded in her temples, her brain quickened and all her senses were alert.

Her heart hammered in her chest as the footsteps came closer and closer, squeaking on the wooden floor.

The only bit of him that was moving was his heart, which pounded so hard it seemed about to break his ribs.

Sweat had collected on his forehead and was trickling down the side of his nose into his eyes. He squeezed them shut and blinked rapidly.

He could hear the voices getting closer. A shiver charged down his spine like an electric shock.

She felt the fear like a coiled spring in the pit of her stomach.

She clenched her teeth so hard her jaw ached.

Clasping her hands in her lap, she moved her lips silently in prayer.

His wide eyes strained to pierce the darkness, darting wildly from side to side, certain they were somewhere nearby.

His voice dropped to an urgent whisper.

He whispered in a tight, choked voice, watching in horror as they moved closer to the stairs.

His voice was hardly more than a whisper from the shadows.

He lingered in the shadows, motionless, alert and ready to move quickly.

She shook from the effort of holding herself still until he passed.

They waited, frozen to the spot, waiting for the thunder of boots on the stairs.

8

Pursued

She sprinted across the street, turned sharp left, charged down the alley, not daring to glance back, just trying to gain as much ground as possible, the **sound of her breath roaring in her ears, her pulse thumping hard**. She didn't dare stop.

Out of the corner of his eye, Tom saw several, scuttling shadows emerging from the end of the passage. **Adrenalin pumping through his veins like molten lava**, he crossed the road as casually as he could, so as not to stand out. Risking just one look over his shoulder, he merged with the crowd.

SECTION 1 – CHARACTERS (VILLAIN/ALLIES)

WORDS

Nouns	**Trail**, road, street, alley, fence, rooftops, corridor, door, window, corner, lift, stairs, escalators
	Ground, floor, surface
	Guard, sentries, men, figures, shadows
	Pursuit, stealth, menace, violence
	Voice, shout, yell, alarm
	Movement, footsteps, feet
	Paces, minutes, seconds
	Smoke, exhaust, smell, fumes
	Car, helicopter
Adjectives	**Dark**, darkened, black-clad, blackened
	Shadowy, ghostly, shrouded

Violent, gruesome, armed

Winding, flying

Burnt, bitter

Verbs	**Tracked**, trailed
	Felt, sensed
	Looked, saw, spotted, spied, noticed
	Silhouetted, flitted, appeared, emerged
	Moved, stood, stepped out, headed, approached, crossed, stopped, blocked
	Spun, swerved, rolled, slid
	Dropped, descended
	Ran, burst, gained, lunged
	Hauled, fished out
	Opened, closed, pointed
	Heard, spoke, shouted, rang, crunched, echoed

PHRASES – NOUNS AND ADJECTIVES

★ On their trail again
★ In pursuit
★ *Out of the corner of her eye*
★ In her periphery
★ *Just a few paces away*
★ Only a stone's throw away
★ Alarmingly close to where . . .
★ *Nearer by the second*
★ Within minutes
★ *Out of nowhere*
★ In front of him
★ Ahead of him
★ Behind him
★ Down the corridor
★ Between the doors
★ In the alley to her left
★ On the street below
★ On the other side of the fence
★ From the landing above
★ Through the streets

* Beside the winding dirt track
* Across the rooftops towards them
* *Several figures*
* Scuttling shadows
* Shadowy figure
* Ghostly silhouette
* Several shrouded figures
* Dark figure
* Two suited men
* Two of them in black
* Black-clad figures
* *Yell of alarm*
* Warning shout behind him
* Guard's voice
* More armed sentries
* *Hiss of the lift doors opening*
* Hurried footsteps
* More feet the other side of the door
* Crunch of a foot on dry bracken and leaves
* *Darkened window*
* Not enough light to see inside
* *Whirr of a large helicopter*
* Black rubber burns on the tarmac surface behind her
* Streaks of burnt rubber
* Bitter smell of exhaust fumes
* Pale blue smoke
* Cloud of exhaust
* Flying stones and clods of earth

PHRASES – VERBS

* Silhouetted against the light
* Spotted a shadowy figure
* Sensed the pursuer
* Flitted across . . .
* Standing at the top of the stairs
* Saw movement to her left
* Caught a flicker of movement
* *Had not heard them approach*
* Had not seen figures rising out of the shadows
* Appeared out of nowhere
* Would soon turn the corner and discover them
* *Raised the alarm*

* Fished out a radio from his pocket and spoke into it
* Could hear shouting behind him
* *Heard them approaching*
* Heard the sound of hurrying footsteps
* Could hear footsteps rapidly approaching
* Heard someone coming into the room
* Heard them heading towards her
* Heard a light step cautiously descending the staircase
* Heard the crunch of a foot
* Bashing at the bushes
* Tried to flush him out
* *Had been spotted*
* Pointed up at him and shouted
* Looking for any movement
* Scanned the forest
* Spying through the window
* *Moving towards him*
* Dropped from the wall
* Began to descend
* Emerged from the shadows
* Approached from all directions
* Heading their way
* Started to gain on them
* Gaining with every step
* Could sense the pursuer closing in on him
* Tracked her across . . .
* *Running up the stairs*
* Burst out of the main building
* Pounded towards her
* Lunged towards the lift
* Running down the corridor towards him
* Sprinted across the courtyard
* *Noticed a car up ahead*
* Parked sideways across the road
* Heard the vehicle approaching before she saw it
* Pulled into the car park
* Pulled silently away
* Spun on the gravel
* Swerved left, bounced back onto the lane
* Skimmed the tops of the trees

Out of the corner of her eye, she saw several, scuttling shadows emerging from the end of the passage.

She caught a flicker of movement. Looking up, she saw him standing at the top of the stairs, silhouetted against the light.

Tom heard someone coming into the room, heard his thudding boots heading towards him.

As she ran, she heard a warning yell . . . she had been spotted. The sentry pointed up at her and shouted.

They dropped down from the wall and came pounding towards her.

The guard stood at the security gate, scanning for any movement.

They were closing in, approaching from all directions, bashing at the bushes, trying to flush her out.

He heard the vehicle approaching before he saw it. It pulled into the car park. No sooner had it stopped, than two, burly, black-clad figures stepped out.

The car raced away, swerving violently left and bouncing back onto the lane, leaving streaks of burnt rubber and the bitter stench of exhaust fumes behind.

SECTION 2 – INTERACTION

Nouns	**Road**, street, alley, corridor, passage, landing, shaft, ledge, rail
	Crowd
	Slope, boulders, rocks, tunnel
	Forest, tree, branch, trunk, foliage, twig
	Ground, floor, building, house, stairs, staircase, room, door, handle, lock, table, chair
	Lift, buttons
	Darkness, shadows, light, torch
	Movement, sound, footsteps, steps, footprints
Adjectives	**Quick**, brisk, fast, urgent, frantic, feverish, desperate, panic-stricken
	Muddy, boggy, slippery, uneven

Verbs	**Closing**, gaining
	Stopped, paused, slowed, walked, headed, followed, reached, retraced
	Joined, crossed
	Grabbed, yanked, hauled, grasped
	Pulled, pushed, tugged, wrenched, wrested, flung
	Dragged, heaved, wedged, propped
	Dived into, scurried along, slipped through, scuttled back, moved back, stepped back, backed away, retreated
	Turned, spun, swung, whirled, swerved, whipped round, jerked, lunged, evaded
	Quickened, hurried, darted, rushed, ran, fled, tore across, piled through, bolted, hurtled, charged, plunged, dashed, sprinted
	Dodged, bobbed, weaved
	Climbed, jumped, leaped, sprang, bounded, pounded, vaulted
	Dropped, crashed, tripped, stumbled, slid, slipped, landed, scrabbled, scrambled
	Crashed through, blundered, shoved, slashed at
	Looked, stared, glanced, searched, peered, peeked, saw, glimpsed
	Heard, banged, slammed

PHRASES – NOUNS AND ADJECTIVES

* ★ For a fraction of a second
* ★ *With a new sense of urgency*
* ★ In this last mad dash
* ★ In one motion . . .
* ★ *Almost at the top, almost safe*
* ★ As they were about to leave the cover of the rocks . . .
* ★ All he had a chance to notice was . . .
* ★ As soon as he was out of sight . . .
* ★ Not sure where it would take her
* ★ *Slowly, noiselessly . . .*
* ★ Nothing to draw attention to herself
* ★ *Middle of the large, bustling crowd*
* ★ Waterlogged trench
* ★ Trailing branches close to the ground

* Towards the trees about a hundred metres away
* Through the twists and turns of the tunnel
* Straight into someone coming from the opposite direction
* *Narrow staircase hidden in the shadows*
* Up the stairs in three quick bounds
* Full of cardboard boxes and wheelie bins
* *Head down, arms pumping*
* A moving target

PHRASES – VERBS

* *Paused, then forced himself to keep moving*
* Slowed to a brisk walk, so as not to stand out
* Crossed the road as casually as he could
* Joined the crowd
* *Sprang to their feet*
* Scrambled to her feet
* Launched himself up from the ground
* Hauled himself to his feet
* *Began backing slowly away*
* Scuttled back to the shadows
* Retraced his steps
* *Headed towards the nearest alleyway*
* When he reached the corner . . .
* Turned sharp left
* Fled in different directions
* Stopped when he reached the bend in the corridor
* Made his way down the passage
* Scurried along the passage
* *Piled through the doorway*
* Slipped through the door
* Pushed open the door and dived into the room beyond
* Barely had time to . . .
* May just make it in time
* Before the door slammed
* *Eased herself sideways*
* Kept the wide trunk between her and the footsteps
* As soon as the footsteps receded . . .
* Without even looking up
* *Knew he had to move quickly*
* Forced himself to move faster
* Tried to gain as much ground as possible
* Tried to put as much distance between her and her assailants

- *Quickened his pace*
- Raced towards . . .
- Darted back into the room
- Bolted up the stairs
- Broke into a run
- Ran blindly on
- Ran on until his lungs were bursting
- Ran for his life, leaving his torch behind
- Began running towards the house
- Started running again, across the street, trying to get out of sight . . .
- Ran faster, pushing herself to the limit
- Bolted round the house and rushed inside
- Ran pell-mell down the slope
- Kept on running, arms pumping, her lungs burning
- Pressed on, running when he could
- Hurtled towards the shadows
- Charged down another alleyway
- Plunged down a huge underground shaft
- Dashed the last few yards
- Tore across the courtyard
- Exploded out through the gate
- Darted across the street, and plunged down the alley
- Turned blindly to the right at the end
- Swerved to the right, down another alley
- *Sprinted for the stairs*
- Bounded down the steps, taking them three at a time
- Pounded down the steps, faster and faster
- Swung herself round flight after flight
- *Darted and dodged through the trees*
- Ran, bobbing and weaving, across the park
- Weaved in and out of the bushes
- Ran again, slashing through the branches, heading for the darkest part of the forest
- Dodged left and right down the warren of corridors
- *Crashed through the undergrowth, stumbling as she ran*
- Shoved the bins out of the way
- Slammed through the gate
- *Stumbled towards the tree she had spotted*
- Blundering and slipping . . .
- Fought his way through the undergrowth . . . grasping at his ankles
- Stumbled on the rutted forest floor
- Tripped over rocks and fallen trees
- Slid on the loose stones
- Slipped into boggy patches and cannoned off tree trunks

* Stumbled over a ledge and hit the ground
* Stumbled on, almost falling on some tree roots
* Landed on his belly, scrabbled up and carried on
* Slipping and sliding in the boggy marsh
* *Recovered his balance and kept running*
* Managed to keep his balance
* *Hauled herself up, edged along*
* Pulled herself up onto the next branch, then the next
* Climbed higher and higher
* Leaped the low stone wall
* Vaulted roots as they went
* Launched himself down the slope
* Dropped the last few metres
* Crashed down on the ground
* Knew that it was a long way to fall if he slipped
* *Let the shadows swallow them*
* Ran the rest of the way, keeping to the shadows of the hedgerow
* Plunged deeper into the forest
* Made another dash for the shadows
* *Prayed that he hadn't been spotted*
* *Spun round*
* Spun on his heel
* Whirled round
* *Gaining on her with every step*
* Closing in on her
* About to turn away when . . .
* Just getting back to his feet when . . .
* Swerved just in time
* Quickly, he jerked back as . . .
* Quickly stepped back
* Managed to evade the man's lunge
* *Had just reached the top of the stairs when . . .*
* Found himself face to face with . . .
* Jumped as someone clapped a hand on his shoulder
* *Grabbed his arm*
* Yanked her onwards
* Pulled her through a doorway
* Dragged her inside
* Grabbed her hand and tugged her along the passage
* *Looked again*
* Stared down
* Turned and saw . . .
* Peered down the stairs
* Turned towards the source of the sound

- ✴ Moved his head very slowly and peered round his cover
- ✴ Got to the cover of the trees and looked back
- ✴ Waited a moment and peered round
- ✴ Risked just one look back over her shoulder
- ✴ Whipped round to see
- ✴ Threw terrified glances over his shoulder
- ✴ Glanced anxiously back at her pursuers
- ✴ Heard a movement and glanced back
- ✴ Didn't dare to turn round
- ✴ *Saw the guard fishing in his pocket*
- ✴ Pulled out his phone, started talking urgently
- ✴ *Could hear…*
- ✴ Heard a twig snap
- ✴ Heard someone coming into the room
- ✴ Banged shut behind them
- ✴ Listened for the sound of approaching feet
- ✴ Couldn't tell where the steps were coming from
- ✴ *Grabbed a chair and wedged it under the door handle*
- ✴ Frantically, tried to double-lock the door
- ✴ Wrenched open the door
- ✴ Yanked at the handle …
- ✴ Grabbed the handle and almost ripped it off its hinges
- ✴ Thumped the buttons on the lift
- ✴ *Used the branch like a carpet sweeper*
- ✴ Swung it rhythmically from side to side
- ✴ Moved backwards along the track to brush away their footprints

SENTENCES

They walked for another ten minutes, neither of them speaking, and then they saw them up ahead.

Kitty whirled round and found herself face-to-face with her assailant.

He was closing in on her. She knew she had to move quickly. Darting towards the door, she yanked at the handle. It was locked.

Swiftly, Rob retraced his steps through the twists and turns of the tunnel.

He couldn't tell where the steps were coming from. He quickened his pace, but the ground was uneven and he stumbled, crashing to the ground.

He glanced anxiously over his shoulder as the steps moved closer. Darting up the stairs, he saw a door ahead and raced towards it. He yanked at the handle; wrenched the door open; dived inside.

Katie hauled herself up onto the ledge, edged along to the rail and grasped it with both hands. She prayed she hadn't been spotted.

Tom crossed the road as casually as he could, so as not to stand out, risking just one look over his shoulder, before he merged with the crowd.

Whirling to the left, she just managed to evade the man's lunge. She sprinted across the street, turned sharp left, charged down the alley, not daring to glance back, just trying to gain as much ground as possible.

She stopped when she reached the narrow track. She had heard something . . . the snap of a twig. She hurtled back towards the trees . . . the safety of the shadows. Easing herself sideways, she kept the wide trunk between herself and the approaching footsteps.

He ran to the next corner, waited a moment, and peered round.

Almost at the top, almost safe . . . almost. He forced himself to move faster, but he also knew that it was a long way to fall if he slipped.

She scrambled to her feet, and began to move, not sure which way to go, only knowing that she couldn't stay where she was.

She had spotted a brief flicker of light on the top of the hill. They were on her trail again. She picked up the branch using it like a carpet sweeper, swinging it from side to side as she moved backwards along the track towards the river.

He darted and dodged through the trees. Blundering and slipping, he fought his way through the undergrowth, which was grasping at his ankles.

She sprinted for the stairs, threw open the door and, using the metal rail, bounded down the steps, taking them three at a time.

She swung herself round flight after flight, pounding down the steps, faster and faster.

Suddenly, she was out in the opening, tearing across the courtyard, exploding out through the gate.

Bent over, she tried to get her breath, risking a glance over her shoulder. They had picked up her trail. She started running again, across the street, trying to get out of sight . . . forcing herself to ignore the burning that was creeping up her legs.

She saw the guard fishing in his pocket and pull out his phone. She had been spotted. Faster and faster she ran, pushing herself to the limit, running blindly on, trying to put as much distance as possible between herself and her assailants.

She ran, bobbing and weaving across the park, towards the trees about a hundred metres away.

She swerved to the right. Down another alley. Cardboard boxes and wheelie bins were strewn across the path. Crashing through the boxes, she stumbled, recovered her balance, shoved the bins out of the way and started running again.

Her eyes darting rapidly from side to side, scanning the street, Katie spotted an alley to her left. She darted across the street, plunged down the alley, turned blindly to the right at the end, not sure where it would take her.

With a new sense of urgency, they plunged deeper into the forest, letting its shadows swallow them.

He launched himself down the slope, sliding on the loose stones, but just managing to keep his balance and surge on.

He rose to his feet, and sprinted to the wall, dropping to his knees behind it.

He leaped the low stone wall, slammed through the gate, weaved in and out of the bushes, desperate to make himself a moving target.

They ran pell-mell down the slope, vaulting roots as they went, moving as quickly as they could.

Never once did she turn and look back . . . just kept on running, arms pumping, her lungs burning.

She was up and running again, slashing through the branches, heading for the darkest part of the forest.

SECTION 3 – REACTION

WORDS

Nouns	**Brain**, heart, pulse, adrenalin, palms
	Fear, terror, dread, panic
	Wince, gasps, tremble
	Guards, sentries
Adjectives	**Shaking**, trembling, unsteady, clumsy
	Tight, rasping, shuddering
	Numb
	Sweaty
Verbs	**Raced**, pounded, hammered, pumped, flooded, blasted
	Gripped, clutched, choked
	Glanced, peered

PHRASES – NOUNS AND ADJECTIVES

* ★ *An explosion of adrenalin*
* ★ *Her palms sweaty, her heart racing*
* ★ *Unsteady, rasping gasps*

PHRASES – VERBS

* ★ As he glanced back . . .
* ★ As the footsteps came closer and closer . . .
* ★ Brain was racing
* ★ Tried desperately to think of . . .
* ★ Fear of being caught
* ★ Thought of what would happen if they caught her
* ★ *Raced through her body*
* ★ Heart almost stopped
* ★ Blasted by an explosion of terror
* ★ Pumped through his veins like molten lava
* ★ *Choked off his breath*
* ★ Breathed heavily
* ★ Gulping for air
* ★ Made her wince and tremble
* ★ Clutched his hand to his mouth
* ★ Stop himself screaming out
* ★ *Choked back the bile that rose in her throat*
* ★ Flooded his face
* ★ Tried to pick up the key, but . . .
* ★ Fingers felt frozen, numb, clumsy

SENTENCES

Her mind was working with feverish haste, trying desperately to think of a way of evading the guards, who were gaining on her every minute.

An explosion of adrenalin raced through her body and she quickened her pace.

The fear of being caught choked off his breath into unsteady, rasping gasps, until he was gulping for air.

When she thought of what would happen if they caught her, she was blasted by an explosion of terror that made her wince and tremble, her palms sweaty, her heart racing.

As he glanced back, his heart almost stopped. They were coming at him from all directions, and closing in on him.

Her heart pounded as the footsteps came closer and closer, squeaking on the wooden floor.

She breathed heavily, choking back the bile that rose in her throat.

Panic flooded his face as he spotted several scuttling figures emerging out of the shadows.

He clutched his hand to his mouth to stop himself screaming out.

He tried to pick up the key, but he was so scared his fingers felt frozen, numb, clumsy.

She started to run, not daring to look back, the sound of her breath roaring in her ears, her pulse thumping hard. She didn't dare stop.

9

Trapped

1. She sprinted down the alley. At the end, she was faced with a high, brick wall. It was another dead end!

    The man emerged out of the gloom, sweeping his torch over the passage. **Her heart missed a beat, squeezed like a vice by her terror.** Suddenly, he swung round, and aimed his torch at where she was crouched in the shadows. **She was rooted to the spot, like a rabbit caught in the headlights. Slowly, she raised her shaking hands in the air in an act of surrender.**

2. A dark figure, wearing a balaclava helmet, stood inside the doorway, only two darting eyes visible through the slits, the rest of his face covered and his voice muffled. When he spoke, the words came rasping out of the darkness. **Her mouth twisted in a scream that never came. She shuddered, went rigid, as if frozen to the spot.** Before she could cry for help, he had clamped a hand over her mouth.

SECTION 1 – CHARACTERS/SETTING

WORDS

Nouns	**Way out**, exit, fire escape, dead-end
	Gate, door, window, stairs, steps, corridors
	Buildings, tent, rooms, basement, dungeons
	Lock, bolt, bars, padlock
	Alley, street, passage
	Trees, undergrowth, foliage, branches, leaves, ditch
	Darkness, shadows, gloom, moonlight

Helmet, balaclava

Torch, light, glare

Silence, footsteps, voices, whisper

Adjectives	**Huge**, muscular, burly, strong, menacing
	Dark, empty, silent, still, echoing, thudding
	Rusty, flimsy
Verbs	**Emerged**, entered, stood, loomed, leaned over, blocked, barred
	Crept, crouched, edged, stole through
	Locked, padlocked
	Heard, thudded, slammed, clicked, whispered
	Wore, dressed

PHRASES – NOUNS AND ADJECTIVES

- ★ Only one exit through the gate
- ★ No windows, no other doors. No escape
- ★ No trees, no buildings to shield them
- ★ Nowhere to hide
- ★ Nowhere to run
- ★ No way out
- ★ *Heavy oak door*
- ★ Flimsy lock of the door to her room
- ★ *Silhouette of a huge, muscular figure*
- ★ Dark shadows
- ★ A figure dressed in black
- ★ More than one of them
- ★ Rustle of bedclothes
- ★ With a soft thud
- ★ *Behind him*
- ★ In front of him
- ★ Through the closed door
- ★ In the small of his back

PHRASES – VERBS

- ★ *Dressed in black*
- ★ Wearing a balaclava helmet
- ★ *Only became aware of him when . . .*

* *Emerged out of the gloom*
* Turned into the alley
* Running down the corridor
* *Had spotted her*
* Blocked the route
* Blocked her escape
* Stood inside the doorway
* *Breaking into the room*
* Forced open the door
* Stealing through the window
* Edged into her room
* Entered his tent
* *Crept up behind him*
* Slipped behind her
* Leaned over her
* Loomed above her
* *Swept his torch over the area*
* Crouched and aimed his torch at . . .
* *Heard the footsteps*
* Thudded up the stairs
* Slammed open
* Came rasping out of the darkness
* Whispered menacingly in the darkness
* Heard a click
* *Padlocked from the outside*
* Barred from the outside
* Covered the windows

SENTENCES

The only exit was through the main gate and the guards were blocking that route.

They had spotted her. She could hear footsteps thudding up the stairs. The fire escape door wouldn't budge. It was padlocked from the outside.

No windows. No other door. No escape. His pursuers were running down the corridor, gaining with every minute that passed. He was trapped.

The man emerged out of the gloom, sweeping his torch over the area. Suddenly, he swung round, crouched and aimed his torch into the undergrowth.

Someone was quietly forcing open the flimsy lock. The door creaked open and she saw the silhouette of a huge, muscular figure edge into the room.

There was a noise outside the door. Someone was in the process of breaking into her room.

The heavy wooden door slammed open, crashing into the wall.

A dark figure, wearing a balaclava helmet, stood inside the doorway, only two darting eyes visible through the slits, the rest of his face covered and his voice muffled. When he spoke, the words came rasping out of the darkness.

SECTION 2 – INTERACTION

WORDS

Nouns	**Eyes**, arm, hand
Adjectives	**High**, low
	Metal, steel, stone, brick, oak, wooden
Verbs	**Locked**, padlocked, trapped
	Stretched out, lunged, seized, grabbed
	Pulled, pushed, tugged, yanked, shoved
	Looked, searched, scanned, swept, shielded
	Aimed, blinded
	Led to, emerged
	Ran, darted, sprinted, tore, advanced, spun around
	Hid, concealed

PHRASES – NOUNS AND ADJECTIVES

* ⋆ Another dead end
* ⋆ No chance of escape
* ⋆ Nowhere else to go
* ⋆ Nowhere to hide
* ⋆ No time
* ⋆ *Up and down stairs*
* ⋆ Through empty rooms
* ⋆ Along the corridor

PHRASES – VERBS

* ⋆ Led to the outside
* ⋆ Trapped in a dead end

* Barred from the outside
* *Swept her eyes around the corridor*
* Scanned the room for an exit
* *Hurtled up the stairs*
* Pounded up and down stairs
* *Sprinted wildly down the corridor*
* Darted along the trail
* Tore through empty rooms
* Dashed to the window
* *Lunged at the door*
* Grabbed the door handle
* Stretched out his hand towards the handle
* Checked every door, every window . . . locked
* Pulled, pushed, tugged at every door
* Dashed to the window, yanked at the handle, pulled, pushed
* Felt around for the stone
* Opened the sliding wooden panel
* *Would not budge*
* Swung open
* Began to open
* *Concealed in the darkness . . .*
* Trapped in a dead end
* Faced with a high, brick wall . . . another dead end
* *Caught Katie full in its glare*
* Threw up her hand to shield her eyes
* *Made a move to roll out of bed and onto the floor*
* Doubted she would have time to unlock the door

SENTENCES

She scanned the room for an exit.

Her eyes swept round the corridor. There was nowhere to hide.

She lunged at the door. It was locked. She was trapped.

Sprinting wildly down the corridor, Kitty pulled, pushed, tugged at every door.

Quickly, she dashed to the window, yanked at the handle. She pulled. She pushed. It was also locked. There was no way of escape.

He was concealed in the darkness, but trapped in a dead end. If his attacker returned, he knew he would have nowhere to run.

She sprinted down the alley. At the end, she was faced with a high, brick wall. It was another dead end.

As he stretched out his hand towards the handle, it turned. Frantically, he tried to find the stone that opened the sliding wooden panel, but there was no time. The door swung open. They were trapped.

Suddenly, the beam caught Katie full in its glare. She threw up her hand to shield her eyes, knowing that there was nowhere to run.

With an explosion of terror, she realised that even if she managed to get close to the door, he had locked and bolted it. She doubted whether she would have time to unlock the door before he caught her.

He opened his eyes as he heard footsteps closing in on him and knew that this was the end.

SECTION 3 – REACTION

WORDS	
Nouns	**Fear**, dread, terror, horror
	Heart, adrenalin, pulse, beat, breath, throat, windpipe, cheeks
	Croak, moan, gasp, whisper, words
	Surrender
Similes/ Metaphors	**Fog**, wave, jaws, rabbit, headlights
Adjectives	**Numb**, tense, rigid, frozen
	Rasping, jagged, strangled, gasping, jumbled
	Cold, icy, chilly
	Shaking, trembling
Verbs	**Tensed**, stiffened, rooted, paralysed, froze
	Swept, surged, seized, stabbed, slithered, crept, twisted
	Lifted, raised, stood
	Shuddered, trembled
	Darted, swept
	Choked, gasped, blew, bubbled
	Drenched

PHRASES – NOUNS AND ADJECTIVES

* Sense of hearing heightened
* A huge wave of adrenalin
* In an act of surrender
* *Frozen with terror*
* As if rooted to the spot
* Like a rabbit caught in the headlights
* *Like a dark fog*
* Fear of where they would take her; what would happen to her
* Hands trembling and her face deathly pale
* *Croak of fear*
* Moan of despair
* Strangled whisper
* Rasping, jagged breath
* Jumbled stream of words, one rushing into the next

PHRASES – VERBS

* It was as if time had stopped
* Surrounded and would not be allowed to escape
* *Swept through her body*
* Seized him in its jaws
* Bubbled in his throat
* Missed a beat
* Squeezed like a vice by her terror
* Stabbed by a splinter of fear
* Slithered around her
* Tried to control her sense of impending doom
* *Jumped every time a sound carried down the corridor*
* Paralysed with fear
* Stood rooted to the spot
* Shuddered and went rigid
* Slithered to a halt
* *Blew out her cheeks to stop herself howling*
* Gasping for breath
* Drew a rasping, jagged breath
* Twisted in a scream that never came
* Opened her mouth to speak
* Froze in her throat
* Shrank into silence
* *Swept over the scene in front of her*
* Darted to and fro

* *Drenched in sweat*
* Brought a damp chill that gradually crept over her
* *Raised her shaking hands in the air*
* Stood with hands on hips, head bowed

SENTENCES

Even though he tried to control his sense of impending doom, deep down he knew . . . he was surrounded and would not be allowed to escape.

She stiffened. She opened her mouth to speak but only a croak of fear emerged.

Lying in bed in the darkness, her sense of hearing heightened, a huge wave of adrenalin swept through her body.

She was paralysed with fear and jumped every time a sound carried down the corridor.

Katie blew out her cheeks to stop herself howling.

Dread seized him in its jaws. The footsteps were ominously close. Panic bubbled in his throat as suddenly he saw them at the end of the corridor.

Her heart missed a beat, squeezed like a vice by her terror. Blowing out her cheeks, she drew a rasping, jagged breath.

Fear slithered around her like a dark fog, bringing a damp chill that gradually crept over her, even though she was sweating and drenched in sweat.

Katie was stabbed by a splinter of fear, fear of where they would take her; what would happen to her.

She was rooted to the spot, hands trembling and her face deathly pale.

Her mouth twisted in a scream that never came. Before she could cry for help he had clamped a hand over her mouth.

Her eyes darted to and fro, sweeping over the scene in front of her. A low moan of despair escaped her lips. She slumped to the floor and shrank into silence.

When she tried to speak, only a jumbled stream of words emerged, one rushing into the next.

She stood rooted to the spot like a rabbit caught in the headlights. Slowly, she raised her shaking hands in the air in an act of surrender.

It was as if time had stopped. She shuddered and went rigid, as if frozen to the spot.

He slithered to a halt and stood with hands on hips, head bowed, gasping for breath.

Part 3
The villain

10

Meeting the villain

1. Hook

A key turned in the door. **Tom's pulse raced.** He didn't have time to turn off the light. **He looked round wildly for somewhere to hide.** Before he had moved more than a few paces, the door swung open.

2. Introducing the villain: appearance

A thickset man in a dark suit stepped into the room. His arms were like bars of iron and he looked like he had the power in his massive shoulders to squeeze all the air from Tom's body and shatter his bones. **Tom's heart was beating painfully fast. A silent scream erupted inside his head, urging him to move.** But the man was blocking the door, and there was no other way out.

3. Hinting that the villain is dangerous

As he caught sight of Tom, the man stared with eyes that sparkled like frost – cold and dangerous. Then, as he noticed the monitor flashing, the man's eyes darkened and seethed with fury.

'What are you doing here?' he barked. His voice was cold, commanding, intimidating.

4. Reaction/interaction

Tom took one step back and then another. He watched the man's every move, **his eyes darting backwards and forwards,** waiting for a chance to charge through the gap. **He was utterly alert. Every nerve in his body straining.**

As the thug lunged towards him, Tom darted out of reach, dived under the table and scrambled on his hands and knees towards the door.

5. Dangerous animals

Its huge jaws were open, two lines of ferocious white teeth waiting to snap shut, clamp down on his arm, his leg . . . drag him under the water.

His wrists and arms were straining to hold on, shaking with the effort. His shoulders were burning. He knew he couldn't hold on much longer. But the reek of the beast's breath . . . the sickly stench of stale fish and decaying meat, metres below him, gave him renewed strength. **He struggled, each effort to find a foothold getting weaker.**

SECTION 1 – THE VILLAIN AND HIS ALLIES

TIP: Remember the aim of an adventure story is to get the reader to root for the hero and to make it as exciting as possible by making the hero face many obstacles and dangers before he succeeds. The more evil, sinister and menacing you can make the villain and his allies, the greater the danger facing the hero.

Dangerous animals can be included as additional obstacles used by the villain. Crocodiles, snakes, scorpions and vicious dogs have been included, but there are many others that can be used. Remember that the animals are obstacles to be overcome, and to increase fear and suspense. To keep the pace of your story, it is better that the hero is threatened by the animals, but finds a way of avoiding the attack and serious injury. It is merely a threat, albeit a very dangerous one!

A. Expressions

WORDS	
Nouns	**Expression**, mask, demeanour, countenance
	Look, gaze, glance, glare
	Smile, grin, smirk, leer, sneer, snarl, grimace
Similes/ Metaphors	**Snake**, carcass, granite
Adjectives	**Empty**, cold, chilly, icy, expressionless

Arrogant, sarcastic

Nasty, cruel, evil, spiteful, callous, vengeful

Fierce, livid, hostile, threatening, vicious, murderous, venomous, malicious, withering

Hideous, monstrous, savage, ghastly, grisly, demonic

Sly, cunning, creepy, furtive, sinister

Verbs   **Glanced**, gazed, stared, glared, glowered

Split, curled, stretched, twisted, twitched, tightened, clenched, grimaced

Shot, directed, trained, spread

PHRASES – NOUNS AND ADJECTIVES

* Steely gaze
* Cold, sinister look
* Icy expression
* Smile as empty as a carcass
* Cold, featureless mask
* Expressionless, granite mask
* *Like a grinning snake*
* Reptilian sneer
* Slow, demonic leer
* Furtive, viperish expression
* *Vicious smile*
* Hideous, savage sneer
* Withering look
* Menace in his face
* *Amused, callous look on his face*
* Unpleasant, sarcastic smile
* Ghastly smile of pretended sympathy
* Dramatic expression of mock concern and sympathy

PHRASES – VERBS

* Expression suddenly changed
* Spread across his face
* *Twisted his lips*
* Twisted into a knowing grin
* Split into a nasty, demonic grin

* Twisted in a malicious smirk
* Stretched his mouth into a grisly smile
* *Stretched in a hideous sneer*
* Glanced demonically
* Smirked satanically
* Bared his yellow teeth
* *Wrinkled with disgust*
* Curled with revulsion
* Snorted with contempt
* Features tightened with contempt
* *Shot him a withering look*
* Directed a look of purest venom
* Trained his steely gaze on her
* Lingered like a scar

SENTENCES

It was difficult to know how he was going to react. His face was an expressionless mask of granite.

The memory of the menace in his face would linger like a scar.

His face wore a cold, featureless mask that offered no hint of mercy.

A malicious smile spread across his face.

His pale, skull-like face split into a nasty, demonic grin.

Her smile was as empty as a carcass.

His mouth twisted into a malicious smirk.

Robert trained his steely gaze on her and stretched his mouth into a grisly smile.

She directed a look of pure venom at his retreating back.

His face suddenly changed to a dramatic expression of mock concern and sympathy.

He had an amused, callous look on his face as he watched Kitty writhing on the floor.

Snorting with contempt, he bared his yellow teeth in a reptilian sneer.

His mouth curled with revulsion as she made a despairing lunge at his arm.

As he opened the door for them to leave, his mouth twisted into a knowing grin.

His icy expression suddenly changed as he curled his lips into a savage sneer.

She took aim with an invisible gun and gave him a slow, demonic leer.

B. Eyes

WORDS

Nouns	**Look**, stare, glare, slits
Adjectives	**Small**, little, beady, buggy, staring, unblinking
	Hard, cold, ice-cold, icy, frosty, steely, flinty
	Sharp, crafty, intelligent
	Evil, cruel, piercing, withering, seething
	Dangerous, vicious, predatory, snake-like, hooded
	Ghostly, monstrous, feverish, demon-haunted, devilish
Verbs	**Stared**, squinted, narrowed, bulged, flickered
	Drilled, blasted, burned, blazed, glinted, sparkled, darkened, pierced

PHRASES – NOUNS AND ADJECTIVES

- ★ Cold, steely grey eyes
- ★ Piercing pale globes
- ★ Bright green eyes
- ★ Dark, hooded eyes
- ★ Glinting black gleam
- ★ No whites in his eyes
- ★ Dark, seething with fury
- ★ Small and hard as raisins
- ★ Buggy, little eyes
- ★ *Frosty and narrowed*
- ★ Cold and malignant
- ★ Slits of fury
- ★ Piercing as razors
- ★ As cutting as a steel blade
- ★ Bulging and fierce in his twisted face
- ★ Eyes like a hawk
- ★ Vicious, predatory stare
- ★ Staring, snake-like eyes
- ★ Intelligent, like the bright eyes of a snake
- ★ Something weird and devilish in his eyes
- ★ Demon-haunted expression
- ★ Not a man to be crossed

* Pair of silver-mirrored sunglasses
* Pair of tinted glasses

PHRASES – VERBS

* Stared with unblinking eyes
* Sparkled like frost – cold and dangerous
* Glinted evilly
* Burned like furnaces
* Burned with a cruel light
* Drilled into her
* Darkened warningly
* Took in every detail, every movement
* Froze her blood

SENTENCES

His stare was as cutting as a steel blade.

Her bright, green eyes burned with cruel light.

She stared with eyes that sparkled like frost – cold and dangerous.

His eyes were dark, seething with fury.

His dark, hooded eyes froze her blood and she was unable to speak.

His eyes narrowed and his face hardened. This was not a man to be crossed.

Her eyes burned with a cruel light in her skull-like face.

She stared with unblinking eyes, but her lips twitched briefly.

His small eyes were as dark and hard as raisins, and had a demon-haunted expression.

Kitty spoke in a ghostly whisper, but her eyes darkened warningly.

As piercing as razors, his steely, grey eyes drilled into her.

Like a hawk, her eyes were unblinking, taking in every detail, every movement.

There was something weird and devilish in her eyes, cold and malignant, intelligent like the bright eyes of a snake.

A pair of silver-mirrored sunglasses shaded his eyes.

There were no whites in her eyes; just a glinting black gleam.

He had unblinking eyes that seemed chiselled from ice.

Normally, she covered her eyes with a pair of dark, tinted glasses. When she took the glasses off, they were the scariest eyes they had ever seen – piercing pale globes that never seemed to blink.

The look he gave her reminded her of a dog's eyes when they were preparing to attack – a vicious, predatory stare.

C. Voice

WORDS	

Nouns	**Tone**, hiss, whisper, growl
	Snort, laughter
	Snarl, shout, yell, screech, shriek
	Rattle, wheeze
Adjectives	**Cold**, icy, chilly, frosty, harsh, sharp, clipped
	Mocking, cruel, spiteful
	Dangerous, threatening, vicious, venomous
	Commanding, intimidating
Verbs	**Sneered**, sniggered, jeered, snorted
	Roared, ranted, boomed, screamed, howled, shrieked, bellowed, stormed, thundered, threatened
Adverbs	**Nastily**, angrily, heatedly, fiercely, furiously, viciously, impatiently

PHRASES – NOUNS AND ADJECTIVES

* Frosty voice
* Firm and chilly
* Cold and cruel
* Ice-cold venom
* Splinter of ice in her voice
* *Ghostly whisper*
* Venomous whisper
* *Menacing, threatening tone*
* Hint of sharpness in his tone
* Tone was precise and chiselled with menace
* Threatening, venomous hiss
* Hard and cold as the blade of a dagger
* Like a razor's edge
* Dry and cruel as the desert wind

* Like a vicious, snarling dog
* *Stifled snort*
* Scornful giggle
* Sneering shout
* Screech like a seagull
* Manic laughter
* A cold, jagged cackle like a rusty saw
* Snort of mocking laughter
* Voice was full of malicious laughter

PHRASES – VERBS

* Responded coldly
* Ordered with a sneer of cold command
* *Added nastily*
* Snarled like a vicious dog
* Said in a low, vicious tone
* Loaded with menace
* *Laughed scornfully*
* Snorted with disgust
* Laughed without a shred of humour
* Sprayed spittle as he spat out the words
* Clicked his tongue impatiently
* *Bored into her like a drill*
* Chilled her to the bone
* Sharp words slashed the air

SENTENCES

His voice was cold, commanding, intimidating.

He was used to giving orders and his tone was firm and cold . . . one that expected to be obeyed without question.

His voice was as hard and cold as the blade of a dagger, and equally as menacing.

The voice was as dry and cruel as the desert wind.

She hissed into his face like a wild-cat.

She snarled at him like a vicious dog.

Every word he spoke dripped with venom and hate.

She drew in her breath through clenched teeth in a venomous hiss.

His voice was like a razor's edge.

His tone was so sharp that the words seemed to slash the air.

She threw back her head and laughed like a screeching seagull.

He laughed a cold, jagged cackle like a rusty saw scraping on metal.

Her voice was something between a whisper and a croak, which sounded like dry, dead leaves rustling together in the wind.

However hard she tried to block it out, his voice bored into her like a drill.

It was a haunting voice, and one that visited her nightly in her dreams – a voice of ice-cold venom.

D. Movement

WORDS	
Nouns	**Figure**, snake, cobra, lizard, cat, panther, bird, peacock
	Shadow, ghost
	Predator, prey
	Knuckles, fist
Adjectives	**Dark**, quiet, silent
	Still, motionless, tense, invisible
	Sly, shifty, furtive
	Quick, alert, deft
	Pecking, scuttling
	Tense, rigid
	Jerky, wild, furious, frantic, feverish
Verbs	**Moved**, glided, ran, strutted
	Leaned, hunched, poised, landed, advanced, thundered, pounced
	Folded, crossed, broadened, jerked, flexed, cracked
	Raised, pointed, shook, waved, pounded
	Dismissed, beckoned

PHRASES – NOUNS AND ADJECTIVES

- ★ Like a dark ghost
- ★ Like a scuttling lizard
- ★ Like a figure carved from stone
- ★ Silent and motionless
- ★ Like a predator scenting its prey
- ★ Like a panther waiting to pounce
- ★ As silent as the shadow of a bird
- ★ Tense alertness
- ★ Tense jerk of his fingers
- ★ Slightly hunched stance
- ★ Broadened shoulders
- ★ Alert to an attack
- ★ Ready to pounce
- ★ A face lost in the shadows

PHRASES – VERBS

- ★ Sat motionless
- ★ Raised to his full height
- ★ Leaned forward menacingly
- ★ Poised on the balls of his feet
- ★ Crouched on the edge
- ★ *Landed quietly like a cat*
- ★ Glided like a shadow
- ★ Moved stealthily
- ★ Glided noiselessly like a dark ghost
- ★ *Advanced slowly*
- ★ Strutted like a peacock
- ★ Ran in pecking strides
- ★ Ran like a scuttling lizard
- ★ Thundered towards him
- ★ *Pounded on the table with his fist*
- ★ Pointed her index finger
- ★ *Flexed his fingers and formed them into a fist*
- ★ Cracked the knuckles of both hands
- ★ Felt the iron strength in the man's grip
- ★ Beckoned them to come to him
- ★ Dismissed them with a wave of her hand

SENTENCES

Silent and motionless, she was like a figure carved from stone.

He stood still and poised like a cobra about to strike.

Katie made no more sound than the shadow of a bird.

Crouched on the edge, he was like a panther waiting to pounce.

She was like a dark ghost gliding smoothly, noiselessly in the shadows.

As quietly as a cat, he landed on the other side of the wall. Immediately, he tensed, poised on the balls of his feet, like a predator scenting its prey.

He advanced slowly towards Robert, a demonic smirk in his piggy eyes.

Kitty leaned forward and grimaced at him malevolently.

He flexed his fingers, formed them into a fist and advanced menacingly.

One of his eyes was half-shut and he took aim at her with an invisible gun.

With a tense jerk of his fingers, he beckoned them to him.

She dismissed them with a wave of her hand.

As he shook Alfie's hand, he felt the iron strength in the man's grip.

His arms were like bars of steel and he looked like he had the strength of a bull elephant as he stood with a slightly hunched stance – as if he was always alert to an attack.

He cracked the knuckles of both hands and his muscles bunched up like coiled wire.

E. Scars

WORDS

Nouns	**Skull**, face, jaw, cheeks, mouth, lip, eye, eyebrows
	Skin, flesh, tissue, folds, lumps, patches
	Width, length
	Sores, blisters, burns, bruise, wound, scabs
	Squint, snarl, grimace
Adjectives	**Red**, pink, black, purple, brown, green, yellow
	Wide, thin, huge, small

Jagged, gnarled

Ugly, horrible, grotesque, hideous, permanent, battle-scarred

Verbs   **Ran**, covered, stretched, pulled, dragged, closed, twisted, squinted, puckered, disfigured

Scarred, burnt, scorched, seared, singed, shrivelled

PHRASES – NOUNS AND ADJECTIVES

- ★ Battle-scarred face
- ★ Thin, jagged scar
- ★ Ugly, wide scar
- ★ Hideous scar
- ★ Scar tissue
- ★ Scar just visible above left eyebrow
- ★ Terribly burnt, puckered skin
- ★ Mass of seared, scarred skin
- ★ Scarred and twisted lip
- ★ Huge, pink patches
- ★ Singed hair and eyebrows
- ★ Peeling skin
- ★ Puckered folds
- ★ Gnarled lump of flesh
- ★ Scar above his left eyebrow
- ★ Width of his jaw
- ★ Length of one side of his face
- ★ Black, empty socket
- ★ Permanent snarl
- ★ Curious squint

PHRASES – VERBS

- ★ Disfigured by a wide scar
- ★ Stretched the width of his jaw
- ★ Ran the length of one side of his face
- ★ Covered his face and skull
- ★ *Disfigured by fire*
- ★ Scorched into huge, pink patches
- ★ Shrivelled into a twisted lump of flesh
- ★ *Squinted from a black socket*
- ★ Pulled downwards by a scar
- ★ Pulled his eye into a curious squint

* Pulled into a permanent snarl
* Closed in the puckered folds of a scar
* Dragged her lip to meet her nostril

SENTENCES

A thin, jagged scar was just visible above his left eyebrow.

One of his cheeks was dragged downwards by an ugly scar.

The scars on his skull were clearly visible through his closely shaved hair.

The skin around one eye had been pulled out of shape and gave her a curious squint.

He had a scarred and twisted lip, which was pulled up to meet his nostril.

The left side of his face was terribly burned. It was a mass of seared skin and scorched in huge, pink patches.

His face had been disfigured by fire. One eye squinted from a black, empty socket. His eyebrows were singed and sprouted at odd angles, and his ear was a shrivelled, gnarled lump.

His face was disfigured by a hideous scar that ran the length of one side of his face and pulled his mouth into a permanent snarl.

His face was a mass of scar tissue, which almost closed one eye in its puckered folds.

He had a sallow, scarred face and the haunted look of someone who had seen many battles.

SECTION 2 – DANGEROUS ANIMALS

A. Dog

WORDS

Nouns	**Jaws**, teeth, gums, legs, eyes, fur
	Saliva, drool
	Guard, chain
Adjectives	**Huge**, massive, enormous
	Black, grey

Savage, fierce, vicious, ferocious, snarling, slavering, sharp, razor-sharp

Hind, front

Verbs   **Bared**, opened, snapped, shut

Growled, snarled, barked, sprayed, dripped

Crouched, crept, crawled, edged

Sprung, leaped, pounced

PHRASES – NOUNS AND ADJECTIVES

* A huge, black guard dog
* Enormous, snarling dogs
* A glinting, black gleam
* No whites in its eyes
* Bristling fur on its neck and back
* Guttural, threatening bark
* Massive, snarling jaws
* Strands of drool
* Slavering jaws

PHRASES – VERBS

* Bared its razor-sharp teeth
* Curled its top lip back
* Revealed flashes of razor-sharp teeth
* Dripped from its jaws
* Snarling and snapping
* Watched his every move
* Edged closer and closer
* Crouched low
* Lunged at her
* Hurtled straight towards him
* Jerked back by the chain
* Reared up on its hind legs

SENTENCES

A huge, black guard dog lunged at her.

The enormous black dog bared its razor-sharp teeth.

Strands of drool dripped from its slavering jaws.

Two huge, razor-sharp teeth curved down over its lower lip.

Its bared teeth were razor-sharp and strings of saliva dripped from its jaws.

A dark shape hurtled straight towards him.

Snarling and snapping, the dog reared up on its hind legs as it was jerked back by the chain attached to the wall.

It moved closer . . . stopped . . . crouched on its front legs. Its hair bristled on its neck and back. Keeping low, it edged closer, stopped again, watching his every move. Its lips were pulled right back as it bared its teeth, and issued a guttural, threatening growl.

B. Scorpion

WORDS

Nouns	**Body**, legs, tail, stinger, tip, barbs, pincers
Adjectives	**Curved**, large, thin, bulbous
	Black, brown, red, green, fluorescent
	Deadly, lethal, poisonous, venomous
Verbs	**Raised**, swished, flicked, crackled

PHRASES – NOUNS AND ADJECTIVES

- ★ Deadly, curved tail
- ★ Deadly stinger at the end of its tail
- ★ Poisoned tip
- ★ Venomous barbs
- ★ Large pincers
- ★ Large, bulbous stinger
- ★ Fluorescent green body
- ★ Long thin tail
- ★ Like a poisoned spear

PHRASES – VERBS

- ★ Curved over its back
- ★ Raised one of its pincers

★ Crackled its pincers
★ Swished its stinger through the air
★ Flicked its stinger

SENTENCES

Its deadly, red tail curved over its back.

The venomous barbs dripped lethal poison.

Its stinger swished through the air and then flicked like a poisoned spear.

It raised one of its powerful pincers, which seemed to crackle as it swiped the air between them.

Its deadly tail had venomous barbs that gleamed menacingly . . . dripping lethal poison.

C. Crocodile

WORDS

Nouns	**Body**, shape, tail, scales
	Head, eyes, snout, jaws, teeth
	Breath, odour, stench, reek, fish, meat
Adjectives	**Evil**, ugly, sinister
	Huge, enormous, vast
	Still, motionless
	Vicious, menacing, ferocious
	Bulging, reptilian, camouflaged
	Writhing
Verbs	**Lay**, lifted, emerged, moved, waddled, slid
	Arched, twisted, sliced
	Reared, hurled, lunged, snapped, clamped, rolled, thrashed, dragged

PHRASES – NOUNS AND ADJECTIVES

* ⋆ Dull, enormous shape
* ⋆ Vast length
* ⋆ Almost twice his size
* ⋆ Protective armour
* ⋆ Streamlined body
* ⋆ Long, spiked tail
* ⋆ Rough scales on its tail
* ⋆ Writhing tip of its tail
* ⋆ Long jaws
* ⋆ Huge jaws
* ⋆ Ugly snout
* ⋆ Two lines of ferocious, white teeth
* ⋆ Bulging, reptilian eyes
* ⋆ Reek of the beast's breath
* ⋆ Sickly stench of stale fish and decaying meat

PHRASES – VERBS

* ⋆ Lay motionless in the water
* ⋆ Could be seen above the surface of the water
* ⋆ Began to stir
* ⋆ Lifted its head
* ⋆ Emerged silently
* ⋆ Waddled a few paces
* ⋆ Slid down the slope
* ⋆ Slithered into the water
* ⋆ Arched up over its back
* ⋆ Twisted and sliced through the water
* ⋆ Reared up out of the water
* ⋆ Waiting to snap shut, clamp down on his arm, his leg . . . drag him under the water
* ⋆ Hurled its weight against the ladder
* ⋆ Thrashed its tail from side to side
* ⋆ Rolled, head shaking violently
* ⋆ Lunged into the air with open jaws
* ⋆ Lunged towards him
* ⋆ Rolled over and over in the water
* ⋆ Cut into the flesh
* ⋆ Slammed its jaws shut
* ⋆ Clamped down

SENTENCES

A dull, enormous shape lay motionless in the water.

It was almost twice his size from its snout to the writhing tip of its tail.

Only its ugly snout and bulging, reptilian eyes could be seen above the surface of the water.

It lifted its head. Its vast length began to stir. It waddled a few paces forward. Without warning, it slid down the slope, its tail arched upwards over its back.

Suddenly, the head of a crocodile reared up out of the water.

There was something really evil about the way it moved – twisting and slicing through the water.

The crocodile reared up, hurling its entire weight against the ladder.

Its huge jaws were open, two lines of ferocious white teeth waiting to snap shut, clamp down on his arm, his leg . . . drag him under the water.

One of the crocodiles lunged towards him. Instinctively, he pulled his legs up, tucking his knees in towards his stomach. He heard the jaws of the animal snap together.

As it wallowed around, the water began to boil.

Rolling over and over in the water, it thrashed its tail. He was too late, too slow. The rough scales on its tail cut into the flesh on Alfie's back.

His wrists and arms were straining to hold on, shaking with the effort. His shoulders were burning. He knew he couldn't hold on much longer. But the reek of the beast's breath . . . the sickly stench of stale fish and decaying meat, metres below him, gave him renewed strength. He struggled, each effort to find a foothold getting weaker.

D. Snake

WORDS

Nouns	**Body**, fangs, teeth, mouth, jaws
	Venom, poison
Adjectives	**Black**, inky, clear
	Poisonous, poison-drenched, venomous
	Quick, fast, lightning-fast
	Sharp, needle-like

Verbs	**Coiled**, uncoiled
	Moved, opened, hyperextended
	Reared, lunged, struck
	Hissed

PHRASES – NOUNS AND ADJECTIVES

* Inky, black jaws
* Poison-drenched fangs
* Like a poisoned demon
* Needle-like teeth
* Drops of clear venom
* Lightning-fast strike
* Awesome power

PHRASES – VERBS

* Uncoiled its body
* Moved so fast it was hard to see
* Reared high off the ground
* Opened its hood
* Hissed savagely
* Opened its inky, black jaws
* Curled its lip back
* Revealed poison-drenched fangs
* Formed on the tips of its fangs
* Hyperextended its mouth
* Struck at his leg
* Sank its needle-like teeth into his boot

SENTENCES

The viper had been coiled in the shadow of the rock.

The snake reared high off the ground.

It opened its inky black jaws.

As its lips curled back, it hissed savagely.

Drops of clear venom dripped from its needle-like teeth.

It lunged at Rob like a possessed demon. It moved so fast it was hard to see.

Lunging at Rob in a lightning-fast strike, it sank its teeth into his boot.

Its poison-drenched fangs hyperextended from its mouth . . . the venom glistening ominously.

E. Black widow spider

WORDS

Nouns	**Body**, legs, spots, glands, fangs, venom
	Web
Similes/ Metaphors	**Dagger**, hypodermic needle, pin-pricks
Adjectives	**Black**, jet-black, red
	Large, shiny
	Sticky, silken
Verbs	**Hung**, lowered, crawled, prickled

PHRASES – NOUNS AND ADJECTIVES

* Above his head
* Large venom glands
* Shiny, jet-black body
* Pair of red spots
* Fangs like a hypodermic needle
* Dagger-like legs

PHRASES – VERBS

* Hung upside down in the centre of the web
* Lowered itself onto his back
* Crawled up his spine towards his neck
* Prickled against his skin

SENTENCES

Above his head was a tangled, sticky, silken web.

Hanging upside down in the centre of the web was a black widow spider.

It had a shiny jet-black body and two red spots.

He glanced at its large venom glands and his stomach lurched.

Its fangs were like hypodermic needles filled with venom.

Something lowered itself delicately onto his bare back.

His skin prickled as it crawled up his spine towards his neck.

Its dagger-like legs were like tiny pin-pricks.

11

Interaction with and reaction to the villain

THE S/C-I-R STRUCTURE

1. **The blood pounded in his temples; his senses were on high alert.** His ears strained for any noise. Nothing. Then suddenly, the silence was shattered by the clanking of the metal shutters as they rolled closed.

    It was as if a lead ball had been dropped in his stomach. There was no other way out. **He tried to clamp down the fear that threatened to paralyse him. He had to move soon or it was all over.**

    In a lightning-fast move, he sprinted across the museum, and charged, head dipped like a raging bull, crashed through his assailants, knocking them to the sides, whirled and dropped to the floor, rolling under the metal shutters. Just in time!

2. Lunging for the lift, she pressed the down button. **She glanced nervously behind her.** No sign of them. **With beads of sweat running down her forehead**, she pressed again. Just then, she heard footsteps thudding across the wooden floor. She pressed again, and again, **not daring to look round.** As the doors finally hissed open, she was gripped by the elbow and hauled backwards.

3. As Tom opened the door and peered inside, long arms locked around him, like the coils of a giant boa constrictor. **Gulping for air**, Tom stamped on the inside of his assailant's foot. As he felt the grip weaken, he lunged forward and sprinted for the door.

4. He sneered at Katie as he sought out a pressure point in her neck. As he pressed down hard, she was instantly paralysed and slumped to the floor, **her face ashen and twisted with pain**.

5.   **She was sweating and burning with rage. The anger had returned like a hard lump at the back of her throat.** In a whiplash move, she lashed out with her feet to take his knees out from under him.

SECTION 1 – INTERACTION

Key points

As he races the villain to complete his task, the hero's role should, where possible, be to:

   ★ avoid detection
   ★ evade capture

Obviously, as an adventure story requires the hero to be in grave danger and up against impossible odds, he will:

   ★ meet the villain and/or his allies, and
   ★ they will attempt to capture the hero to stop him completing the task.

Remember – the type of attack by the villain will depend on the age of the hero:

   ★ Younger heroes are likely to be grabbed, lifted and held when they are captured.
   ★ Older heroes might experience more aggression.

Make sure your action scenes are realistic!
For the reader to *root for the hero*, he needs to demonstrate his courage, resourcefulness and intelligence to overcome the villain, not the 'violence' which is displayed by his opponent. Clever devices, for example, those in the *Alex Rider* series, are useful for the hero, as are skills in:

   ★ Kickboxing
   ★ Martial arts
   ★ Wrestling

Remember – another main element of an adventure story is the triumph of *good over evil*. It is difficult to show the hero as representing *good* if he is armed with a gun or a knife.

The pace needs to be fast when the action takes place, so include:

★ **a mixture of short and long sentences** (readers tend to read longer sentences with multiple clauses faster than short sentences)
★ **short words** (longer words slow it down)
★ **several verbs** in a sentence. For example *He slipped and stumbled, staggered … crashed to the floor.*

A. Movement

WORDS	
Nouns	**Enemy**, opponent, attacker, assailant, pursuer
	Guard, sentry, thug, villain
	Shoulder, back, knees, feet, step, paces
	Ground, floor, mud, door, wall, window
	Obstacle, table, chair, tree, hedge
Similes/ Metaphors	**Cat**, scorpion, snake, cobra
Adjectives	**Right**, left, forwards, backwards, sideways, upwards, downwards
	Low
	Quick, fast, swift, lightning-fast
	Wild, flailing
	Nimble
Verbs	**Stepped**, advanced, circled, closed, intercepted, retreated
	Rushed, dashed, ran, raced, darted, bolted, charged, bounded, sprinted
	Launched, lunged, hurled, plunged
	Jumped, leaped, scaled, sprang
	Swayed, weaved, danced
	Turned, twisted, spun, whirled, twirled

Dodged, ducked, dived, rolled, somersaulted

Dropped, crouched, sunk, flattened

Crept, crawled, slithered

Fell, stumbled, tumbled, slipped, flailed, scrambled, staggered

Collapsed, crashed, toppled

Adverbs　　　**Quickly**, nimbly, desperately, wildly

Nervously, carefully, cautiously, warily, instinctively

PHRASES – NOUNS AND ADJECTIVES

* ✶ Out of reach
* ✶ At the very last second
* ✶ *In a nimble move, she . . .*
* ✶ Whiplash movement
* ✶ Impressive turn of speed
* ✶ Fast as an adder
* ✶ Faster than a rattlesnake
* ✶ Outstretched leg

PHRASES – VERBS

* ✶ Stepped to the side
* ✶ *Stepped back*
* ✶ Took one step back and then another
* ✶ Backed further away
* ✶ *Stepped closer*
* ✶ Moved forward cautiously
* ✶ Advanced again
* ✶ Closed the gap in three paces
* ✶ Circled him warily
* ✶ *Rushed to the door*
* ✶ Raced forward
* ✶ Ran between
* ✶ Darted out of reach
* ✶ Charged through the gap
* ✶ *Lurched across the table*
* ✶ Launched himself upwards
* ✶ Lunged to the right
* ✶ Hurled himself to the side to avoid . . .
* ✶ *Bounded over*

- ★ Jumped over the log
- ★ Cleared the obstacle with ease
- ★ *Sprang to his feet*
- ★ Leapt to her feet
- ★ Sprang up from the ground like a cat
- ★ Leaped nimbly forwards
- ★ Broke into a running leap, arcing high above his opponent
- ★ *Weaved as she ran*
- ★ Swayed to the right
- ★ Swayed out of the way
- ★ Danced to the side in an impressive turn of speed
- ★ *Twisted round*
- ★ Spun quickly and pitched to one side
- ★ Spun round at lightning speed
- ★ Turned nimbly to . . .
- ★ *Ducked below his shoulder*
- ★ Ducked instinctively
- ★ Dodged and weaved
- ★ Lurched sideways to avoid . . .
- ★ *Dropped to his knees and rolled sideways*
- ★ Crouched low and crept towards . . .
- ★ Sunk into a low crouch
- ★ Poised, crouching slightly
- ★ Crouched like a cat about to pounce
- ★ *Slithered like a snake*
- ★ *Dived to the floor*
- ★ Made a dive for the . . .
- ★ Rolled to his feet
- ★ Rolled away as soon as he hit the ground
- ★ Rolled backwards onto her shoulder
- ★ Rolled herself over and stumbled to her feet
- ★ Rolled under the flailing weapon
- ★ Let her momentum carry her into a backward roll
- ★ Somersaulted through the air
- ★ *Threw him off balance*
- ★ Stumbled forward
- ★ Staggered backwards
- ★ Fell forwards with a jolt
- ★ Tumbled forwards, hands reaching out to break her fall
- ★ Toppled backwards
- ★ Flailed wildly
- ★ Crashed headlong into . . .
- ★ Slipped on the muddy ground
- ★ Scrambled to his feet

- ⋆ Struggling, scrambling to find his feet
- ⋆ Collapsed on to his back

SENTENCES

She hurled herself to the side.

She did a backwards roll and sprang to her feet.

At the very last second, she spun round at lightning speed.

She spun quickly, jumped over the log, launched herself towards the overhanging branch and pulled herself up. Just in time!

Rob ran, darting left and right, twisting and dodging, as his pursuer advanced again.

Darting out of his reach, she dived under the table and scrambled on her hands and knees towards the door.

Cautiously, she rolled to her feet, watching his every move, waiting for a chance to charge through the gap.

As his leg shot out to trip her, she tumbled forwards, hands reaching out to break her fall.

Nimbly, Kitty dodged to the right, but missed her footing and crashed headlong into the table.

She swayed out of the way, slipped on the muddy ground, and toppled backwards with a thud.

As she fell, he stepped forward, closing the gap in barely three paces, crouched like a cat about to pounce.

For older heroes

She ducked and weaved, dodging the metal blade, darting out of reach.

She crouched low behind the car as bullets raked the ground around her.

B. Wrestle

WORDS

Nouns	**Force**, strength, grip, armlock, headlock
	Movement, balance, stance, defence, riposte
	Body, chest, back, middle, waist, hip, limbs

Shoulder, arms, forearm, elbow, wrist, hand, fingers, thumb, legs, feet, calf

Head, neck, ears, nose, mouth

Joints, flesh, muscles, biceps, nerves

Floor, ground, table, chair, tree, log, rock, stones

Similes/ Metaphors	**Snake**, python, adder, boa constrictor
	Iron, steel, train
	Bull, bear-hug, rag-doll
Adjectives	**Fast**, speeding, lightning-fast
	Fierce, vicious, thrashing, vice-like
	Whiplash, bone-cracking
Verbs	**Reached**, grabbed, grasped, caught, seized
	Held, gripped, clutched, wrapped, tightened, locked, clamped, pinned
	Pulled, yanked, hooked, twisted, pressed, dug
	Pushed, shoved, dragged, flipped, threw
	Lifted, raised, hauled, hoisted, levered
	Charged, lunged, crashed, smashed, thudded, barrelled, clattered
	Struggled, resisted, fended off, wriggled, writhed, arched, bucked, squirmed, jerked, thrashed, kicked, clawed, thrust
	Swayed, whirled, ducked, slithered, rolled

PHRASES – NOUNS AND ADJECTIVES

* For a moment
* At the very last second . . .
* *Combat stance*
* In a nimble move, he . . .
* Whiplash movement
* Lightning-fast riposte
* *Muscles like ropes of steel*
* Bone-cracking bear-hug
* Force of a speeding express train
* Deadly as a striking snake
* Like the coils of a giant boa constrictor

* Strength of an anaconda
* *Face down*
* Great force against his back and head

PHRASES – VERBS

* *Seized him from behind in a headlock*
* Locked Rob's head under the crook of his elbow
* Jerked the heel of his palm upwards into a vicious lock
* Clamped his right forearm round the back of Rob's neck
* Grasped his shoulders in a grip of iron
* Clamped his hand over her mouth to stop her from screaming
* *Gripped him by the elbow*
* Grabbed his hand
* Grasped his wrist
* Twisted his arm into a lock
* Rotated his wrist painfully
* Dug painfully into the flesh on her arm
* Grabbed both her upper arms with vice-like fingers
* Twisted the arm straight
* Grabbed his thumb and bent it backwards
* Twisted the man's grip, clasping his fingers and rotating them against their joints
* *Clutched his ankle*
* Wrapped his arms around his legs
* Pulled his legs out from under him
* Hooked a foot around one of his legs
* Hooked his right leg behind Kitty's left calf
* *Wrapped an arm around Kitty's middle*
* Grasped him in a bone-cracking bear-hug
* Locked him in a fierce embrace
* Long arms locked around him
* *Yanked her to her feet*
* Hauled her upright
* Lifted her from the ground as if she were a rag-doll
* *Pushed him backward*
* Barrelled into him
* Charged, head dipped like a bull
* Crashed through them
* Knocked them to the sides
* Clattered into him with the chair
* Ducked and hit hard with her shoulder
* Leaped on him and sent him crashing to the floor
* Thudded into the back of his leg

- ★ Pushed him hard in the small of his back
- ★ Crashed down on her
- ★ Lunged like an adder striking its prey
- ★ *Sent him sprawling*
- ★ Threw him off balance
- ★ Flung him backwards into the door
- ★ Drove her face-first into the ground
- ★ Knocked the man to the floor, winding him temporarily
- ★ Smashed to the ground in a tangle of thrashing limbs
- ★ *Struggled, bucking against his body*
- ★ Wriggled like a python
- ★ Slithered out of his grip
- ★ Tried to resist, pulling away from the hands that grabbed at him
- ★ Swaying and twisting, they stumbled across the room
- ★ Thrashed wildly with both feet
- ★ Kicked and clawed and struggled
- ★ Writhed like a snake . . . gripped the ground with his back and legs . . . turned him over
- ★ Bucked and writhed and squirmed against the weight
- ★ Arched with his back, pushing with the balls of his feet to form a bridge with his body
- ★ Created a gap between his back and the floor
- ★ *Felt his grip fail*
- ★ Brought up both arms to break his grip
- ★ Let his body go limp . . . the guard lost his grip for just a second . . . twisted round and lurched forward
- ★ Whirled and dropped to the floor
- ★ Crouched low, grabbed him around the waist
- ★ *Twisted her hip into him, flipping him to the floor*
- ★ Rolled backwards, pulling his assailant on top of him . . .
- ★ Thrust his foot into his stomach, flipping him in an arc over his head

SENTENCES

In a whiplash movement, he grabbed Katie's arm, hauled her to her feet and dragged her out of the door.

As he emerged from his hiding place, he was seized viciously from behind in a headlock.

Alfie caught her by the wrist and dug painfully into the flesh on her arm as he pushed her forward.

He wrapped an arm around Kitty's middle and clamped a hand over her mouth to stop her from screaming.

Grabbing his arm, rotating it painfully, Trish twisted it into a lock, and made him howl in agony.

Mustering all her strength, Kitty writhed like a snake, gripped the ground with her back and legs, and flipped him over.

He charged at him, head down and shoulder dipped, barrelled into his stomach and wrapped his arms around his legs. They hit the ground in a tangle of thrashing limbs.

Trish grabbed the metal trolley. Charged at the guard. As the trolley thudded into the back of the man's leg, he lurched forward into the door.

Rob let his body go limp. The guard lost his grip for just a second. That was all it took. Rob twisted round and lurched forward out of his reach.

Kitty crouched low, grabbed him around the waist, twisted her hip into him and flipped him to the floor.

He hooked his right leg behind Kitty's left calf and sent her crashing to the floor.

Rob rolled backwards, pulling his assailant on top of him, then thrust his foot into his stomach, and flipped him in an arc over his head.

Quickly, Rob dropped down, then threw himself forward, ducking underneath the man's arm.

Trish lashed out with her feet to take his knees out from under him.

With lightning speed, Trish burst from the shadows, clattering into him with the chair, sending the huge man toppling to the floor.

While he was off balance, Trish shoved him backwards, grabbed the box and ran towards the river.

C. Strike

WORDS	
Nouns	**Shoulders**, arm, elbow, hand, fist, palm, fingers
	Leg, hips, knee, foot, heel
	***Attack**, punches, kicks, blocks, chop, strike*
	Head, face, jaw, cheek, neck, throat, windpipe, nose
	Back, chest, ribs, stomach, solar-plexus
	Ground, floor
Adjectives	**Hard**, lethal, vicious, menacing, devastating, explosive, thunderous
	Low, high, flying, spinning

Verbs	**Blocked**, raised, sought, swept, swung, jerked
	Caught, hooked, grabbed, pressed
	Struck, slammed, knocked, punched, snapped, crunched, elbowed, kicked
	Stood, poised, reared, dropped, hopped, spun, pivoted, twisted, faked
	Threw, launched, thrust, drove, delivered, rammed, followed-through, lashed out
	Stuck out, tripped
	Fell, stumbled, toppled, staggered, crashed
	Jumped, leaped, landed
	Immobilised, paralysed

PHRASES – NOUNS AND ADJECTIVES

* In a flash . . .
* Flurry of punches and kicks
* Blistering combination
* With all her strength
* *Karate blow*
* Reverse punch
* Flying chop
* Vicious lock
* Bullet-hard jab
* Knife-hand strike
* Right-hand elbow strike
* *Powerful, roundhouse kick*
* Spinning, hook-kick
* Lethal, flying side-kick
* Explosive back kick
* Low kick to his left leg
* Snap-kick
* *Kick to his chest*
* Right shin
* Straight into his face
* Squarely in the back

PHRASES – VERBS

* ⋆ Poised in a low, cat-like stance
* ⋆ Stood in combat stance
* ⋆ Weight spread evenly over her feet
* ⋆ *Blocked his hand*
* ⋆ Fended him off with . . .
* ⋆ Met the attack
* ⋆ Followed through with a . . .
* ⋆ Drove him back
* ⋆ Aimed for his head
* ⋆ *Jumped high in the air*
* ⋆ Launched himself into a flying jump kick
* ⋆ *Hopped to the side*
* ⋆ Swung round
* ⋆ Spun on her heel
* ⋆ Pivoted on her supporting foot
* ⋆ *Raised a hand*
* ⋆ Brought his arm down in a snapping arc
* ⋆ *Snapped her knee upward*
* ⋆ Brought up his legs
* ⋆ Reared back to kick him in the . . .
* ⋆ Swung her hips round in a circular motion
* ⋆ *Lashed out like a viper*
* ⋆ Lashed out with a flurry of punches and kicks
* ⋆ Jerked the heel of his palm upwards
* ⋆ Sought out a pressure point in his neck
* ⋆ Pressed down hard
* ⋆ Hit him with a knife-hand strike
* ⋆ Swung his hand like an axe
* ⋆ Slammed backwards with his left elbow
* ⋆ Stabbed out with stiffened fingers
* ⋆ Sidestepped and fired a reverse punch
* ⋆ *Lashed out with his foot*
* ⋆ Faked a front kick
* ⋆ Kicked out with all his strength
* ⋆ Charged in with a side-kick
* ⋆ Snapped a roundhouse kick to the stomach
* ⋆ Thrust a low, front kick into . . .
* ⋆ Twisted his body round in a fast knee strike
* ⋆ Side-kicked him in the . . .
* ⋆ Punched forwards into a flying side-kick
* ⋆ *Caught him in the face*
* ⋆ Caught him in the throat

- ★ Drove the heel of his hand into . . .
- ★ Elbowed the guard in the stomach
- ★ Kicked him hard in the knee
- ★ Slammed his foot into his . . .
- ★ Struck the solar plexus
- ★ Smashed into Rob's windpipe
- ★ Rammed into the man's stomach
- ★ Launched a thunderous kick to his . . .
- ★ Crunched into his cheek
- ★ Kicked him squarely in the back
- ★ Grabbed his nose and twisted hard
- ★ Paralysed with pain
- ★ *Crashed to the floor*
- ★ Fell to the ground
- ★ Staggered back

SENTENCES

He was poised in a low, cat-like stance.

Without warning, he lunged at Andrew with a flurry of punches and kicks.

As he moved forward, Kitty held her ground, watching, anticipating the lethal side-kick he was about to aim at her head.

At the last moment, Trish hopped to the side and delivered a roundhouse kick to his stomach.

He made a grab for Katie's arm. Quickly, she pulled her arm back and aimed a kick at his shin.

They started to back away as Rob floored the first guard with a blistering combination of jabs, a spinning back fist and a powerful roundhouse kick.

He jerked the heel of his palm upwards into a vicious lock.

Trish fended him off with a powerful kick to the chest, and swept her hand across in a combined block and knife-hand strike.

Gail elbowed the guard as hard as she could in the stomach and as he doubled over, she dropped to the ground and hooked his leg from behind.

Catching hold of an overhanging branch, Tom launched himself into the air and delivered a flying side-kick at his head.

He sneered at Rob as he sought out a pressure point in his neck. As he pressed down hard, Rob was instantly paralysed and slumped to the floor.

Rob hopped to the side, and as the man came at him again, he jumped high in the air and threw a flying side-kick at his chest.

The guard lunged towards him, lashing out with a flurry of punches and kicks. Rob dodged and weaved, faked a front kick and then, at the last moment, swung round and slammed his foot into his solar plexus in a lethal side-kick.

SECTION 2 – REACTION

Key points

The hero will experience many emotions during the struggle with the villain, including determination, fear, anger and pain. It is not possible in this chapter to include comprehensive vocabulary for all these emotions, otherwise it would be too large to be useful. The majority of the vocabulary is, therefore, based on fear. The general *Descriptosaurus* includes a full section on all of these emotions.

WORDS	
Nouns	**Fear**, dread, terror, horror, panic, turmoil, despair
	Anger, rage, fury
	Nerves, instinct, realisation
	Look, expression, eyes
	Tone, whisper, murmur
	Howl, yell, scream, shriek
	Danger, menace, violence, isolation
Similes/ Metaphors	**Tidal wave**, explosion, tsunami, blanket, fog
Adjectives	**Numb**, sick, raw
	Urgent, desperate, feverish
	Alert, tense, strained
	Wide, round, staring, horror-struck
	Low, tight, choked, strangled, faltering
	High, high-pitched, piercing
Verbs	**Was aware**, knew, feared
	Swept, surged, engulfed
	Screamed, warned, urged

Clenched, gritted

Narrowed, widened, snapped open, fixed, blinked, flicked, flickered, darted

Lowered, shrank

Gripped, crushed

Froze, paralysed, rooted

PHRASES – NOUNS AND ADJECTIVES

* Already too late
* *First flicker of fear*
* Sick with fear
* Blanket of panic
* In a blind panic
* Sheer terror
* Explosion of fear
* Tsunami of fear
* *Every nerve in his body*
* Utterly alert
* All his instincts
* Raw instinct
* Rising sense of danger
* Ominous realisation of the dangerous nature of his task
* Feeling of isolation
* *Look of sheer terror*
* Pinched with terror
* Urgent and anxious
* Startled look
* *Wide eyes*
* Round with terror
* Alert and strained
* Staring and horror-struck
* *Strangled whisper*
* Faltering tone
* Piercing yell
* High-pitched howl
* High, piercing scream
* Full of despair
* *Burst of fury*
* Like a hard lump at the back of her throat
* With a howl of rage

PHRASES – VERBS

* Feared the worst
* Swept through him like a tidal wave
* Settled on him like a dark fog
* Surged through her
* Engulfed him
* *Knew he had to go on no matter what*
* Screamed at him to . . .
* Warned him not to . . .
* Urged his body to move
* Wanted to turn and run
* *Wore a startled expression*
* Clenched his jaw
* (Cold sweat) poured down his face
* *Widened in horror*
* Snapped open in panic
* Narrowed his eyes warily
* Blinked rapidly
* Kept her eyes fixed to the floor
* Flicked from one to the other
* Darted backwards and forwards
* Swept over the scene in front of him
* *Lowered his voice*
* Shrank into silence
* Froze in her throat
* *Gripped his knuckles until they turned white*
* Crushed her nails into the palms of her hand
* *Turned her to stone*
* Stood rooted to the spot
* *Made his cheeks burn*
* Sweating and burning with rage
* Launched himself into the air and delivered a flying side-kick

SENTENCES

She almost jumped out of her skin as she turned the corner and came face-to-face with a guard.

She wanted to turn and run, but knew that she couldn't.

He tried to clamp down the fear that threatened to paralyse him. This was going to be the fight of his life. If they caught him, there would be no escape.

As panic seized his senses, a silent scream erupted inside his head, urging him to move. But it was already too late!

Her mind was reeling as a tsunami of fear engulfed her.

Raw instinct took control. He was utterly alert. Every nerve in his body straining to breaking point.

Suddenly, he knew that he faced great danger. His instincts were on high alert as adrenalin pumped through his body.

Fear choked him with its murderous hands. It gripped at his throat and strangled his breath into deep, unsteady gasps.

Dread seized him in its jaws and panic bubbled in his throat, until he was gulping for air.

She was struck dead with terror. Her heart was beating painfully fast and banged against her ribs.

Her heart missed a beat, squeezed like a vice by her fear. Blowing out her cheeks, she drew a rasping, jagged breath and tried to dampen the sense of impending doom. She couldn't give in now.

She could feel the panic as a prickle at the bottom of her spine.

Her eyes swept over the scene in front of her as she tried to anticipate his next move.

Her face was expressionless, but inwardly she was fighting to remain calm.

Drenched in sweat and heart pounding, Kitty kept her narrowed eyes on him, watching his every move.

He circled them warily, his eyes flicking from one to the other.

Every bone in his body was tensed and the skin tingled at the back of his neck, warning him to be alert.

His wide eyes strained to pierce the darkness and darted wildly from side to side.

It was as if time had stopped. She shuddered and went rigid, as if rooted to the spot.

He shuddered and tensed as a hard ball of determination tightened in his stomach.

She was sweating and burning with rage. The anger had returned like a hard lump at the back of her throat. In a whiplash move, she lashed out with her feet to take his knees out from under him.

A burst of fury made his cheeks burn. With a howl of rage, he launched himself into the air and delivered a flying side-kick.

12
Captured

1. The lights flicked off, leaving her in total darkness. Suddenly she knew she was in real danger. She couldn't see or hear anything, but she sensed them . . . knew they were in the shadows waiting for her. **Every nerve in her body warned her not to move, not to make a sound.**

    Rooted to the spot, her eyes flickered backwards and forwards, desperately trying to pierce the darkness. The only sound was her own ragged breathing. It was too quiet! Where were they?

    There was a sudden shift in the shadows, a creak of a floorboard, but before she could move, a hand grabbed hold of her from behind, and she felt a hard, cold jab in her ribs. Her assailant caught hold of her arms viciously and wrenched them in a lock.

    She was sweating and burning with rage. The anger had returned like a hard lump at the back of her throat. She lashed out with her feet, but no matter how hard she tried she could not break his grip.

2. She gagged as one man pressed a dirty cloth, reeking of petrol, to her mouth, and then tied it at the back of her head. The other man began tying her hands behind her back with nylon cord. Between them, they hauled her down the stone steps and pushed her into the cellar. **Her face was shadowed with misery and regret as she stared at the ground in front of her.** How different things would have been if she had turned back. She tried to wriggle her hands free of the ropes, but they were too tight. **Defeated, she slumped down, fighting back the tears.**

SECTION 1 – CHARACTERS

WORDS

Nouns	**Head**, face, throat, mouth, lips, shoulder, arms, hands, back, spine, ribs, sides, legs, ankles
	Corridor, passage, trail, wall, door, fire escape
	Bed, armchair, chair, steps, floor, ground
	Boot, car
	Cord, cloth, scarf, chain
Adjectives	**Cold**, hard, solid, blunt, rough, smooth
	Stone, metal, nylon
Verbs	**Grabbed**, grasped, caught, clamped, jammed, jabbed
	Pushed, pressed, shoved, pulled, yanked, dragged, bundled
	Covered, wrapped, tied, bound, held, pinned

PHRASES – NOUNS AND ADJECTIVES

* Nylon cord
* A strip of dark cloth
* Clanging of a heavy chain

PHRASES – VERBS

* Wrenched the phone out of his hands
* Grabbed hold of him from behind
* Slammed into his back
* Pressed into her spine
* Shoved him in the small of his back
* Felt something blunt and solid
* Felt a jab in the ribs
* Wrapped a hand around her shoulders
* Jammed into the back of his head
* Before he could scream for help
* Grabbed him by the throat
* *Caught hold of her arms*
* Lunged and caught her arm
* Put them in a lock

- ☆ Pinned her arms to the sides
- ☆ Tied her hands behind her back
- ☆ *Clamped over her lips*
- ☆ Smothered her mouth
- ☆ Clamped across his mouth
- ☆ Gagged him
- ☆ Felt the rough hand go over his mouth
- ☆ Tied a scarf around her mouth
- ☆ Tied it at the back of her head
- ☆ Covered the lower half of her face
- ☆ Stopped her shouting out
- ☆ *Pulled over her head*
- ☆ Pushed her head down
- ☆ Yanked away from her head
- ☆ *Held her legs*
- ☆ Bound her ankles
- ☆ Locked around his ankle
- ☆ *Pushed her into an armchair*
- ☆ Pushed up against a cold wall
- ☆ Dragged forward
- ☆ Dragged barefoot down the corridor
- ☆ Manhandled across the room
- ☆ Guided him, still blindfolded, down the . . .
- ☆ Bundled her into the boot of the car

SENTENCES

Strong arms grabbed him from behind.

Before he could cry out for help, they had gagged him.

The men shoved him in the small of the back towards the cell.

The words came rasping out of the darkness. He hadn't heard them coming and now it was too late. He felt a hand grab hold of him from behind.

Someone slipped behind her and grabbed her by both arms, pressing against her so she could barely move her feet.

He kneed her in the back of the leg so she had no choice but to move forward.

He was manhandled across the room and pushed against a cold wall. A metal cuff was locked around his ankle and he heard the clanging of a heavy chain from the wall behind him.

From the slither of moonlight stealing through the narrow, barred windows, he could just make out someone leaning over him, and then he saw a glint of metal.

He hadn't noticed the other man who had crept up behind him. A hand suddenly wrenched the phone out of his hands and as he turned back, he felt a hard, cold jab in his ribs.

His hand smothered her mouth and pushed her head down heavily against the pillow.

The men shoved him in the small of his back, sending him stumbling towards the dungeon.

He neither heard nor saw the man enter his tent. The first time he became aware of his presence was when he felt a hand clamped across his mouth.

One hand was clamped over her mouth, the other wrapped round her shoulder and she was bundled into the boot of the car.

Whilst one man began tying her hands behind her back with nylon cord, the other held her legs, and bound her ankles. A scarf was tied around her mouth to stop her shouting for help.

As she stumbled, something cold and hard was pressed into her spine, warning her to move forward.

They caught hold of his arms and put them in a lock, then dragged him barefoot down the corridor, through a fire escape door, and out into the dark, cobbled alley and the chill of the night.

As she was shoved into the basement, the door was slammed shut, and she heard a click as it was locked.

The footsteps echoed in the silence, and gradually died away until there were no more footsteps. Silence. Throbbing silence. She was alone.

SECTION 2 – INTERACTION

WORDS

Nouns	**Grip**, bindings, rope, cord, chain
	Window, door, floor, lamp
	Undergrowth, tree, sapling
	Hands, wrists, legs, shin, knees, feet, ankles, heel
Adjectives	**Strong**, powerful
	Cold, concrete, marble
	Tight, dark, silent
	Desperate

Verbs	
	Loosened, freed
	Lifted, raised, carried
	Catapulted, flew, hung, swung
	Struggled, fought, twisted, jerked, wriggled, writhed, bucked, thrashed, kicked, slammed
	Turned, ran, sprinted, darted
	Moved, inched, shifted, shuffled, slid
	Stumbled, toppled, slumped
	Grasped, held, pulled, yanked
	Shouted, screamed, yelled, shrieked
	Banged, hammered, pounded
	Blinked, woke
	Closed, locked

PHRASES – NOUNS AND ADJECTIVES

* One minute they were . . . and the next . . .
* For a moment
* Her first thought was to . . .
* Now it was too late
* Until someone came to let her out
* *No matter how hard she tried*
* Too strong
* Too tight
* *Against her captor's grasp*
* Impossible to free or even loosen the bindings
* With her hands and feet bound . . .
* Rope around his wrists
* Around her hands and feet
* Cold, concrete floor
* No more footsteps. Silence. Throbbing silence
* *Dark when he woke up*
* Dark outside

PHRASES – VERBS

* *As the door closed*
* *Turned to flee*
* Sprinted towards some undergrowth

★ *Attached to a tree sapling*
★ Catapulted him off his feet
★ Flew into the air
★ Hung there, swinging like a bag of coconuts
★ *Jerked back but it was too late*
★ Twisted round, trying to break free
★ Tried to fight back
★ Struggled, but she was held fast
★ Writhed and bucked
★ Thrashed and kicked
★ Thrashed, but the arms holding her were too powerful
★ Tried to wriggle her hands free of the ropes
★ Kicked out, slamming a heel into his shin
★ Could not break his grip
★ *Knew it was hopeless*
★ Looked at each other desperately
★ Tried to focus on . . .
★ *Nodded that she would not scream for help*
★ Removed his hand that had been clamped over her lips
★ *Shoved forwards and stumbled on reluctantly*
★ Lifted off her feet and carried back
★ *Pulled over her head*
★ Yanked away from her head
★ Blinked in the dazzling light
★ *Moved in single file*
★ Inched her way to the door
★ Shuffled over to the window
★ Shuffled and slid on the wooden floor
★ Slumped down, fighting back the tears
★ Slid down on his knees on the . . .
★ Toppled forward onto his knees
★ Lay on his back, staring into blackness
★ *Struggled to grasp the marble lamp*
★ Managed to hold on to it
★ Waited for the door to open
★ *Screamed and shouted and hammered on the door*
★ Pounded on the metal door with his fists
★ Closed behind her, and locked
★ Closed her eyes
★ *Wondered how long he had been held captive*
★ Stayed together to share their warmth

He hadn't heard him coming and now it was too late.

She screamed again as she was lifted off her feet and carried back. She kicked out, slamming a heel into his shin.

No matter how hard she tried she could not break his grip.

Katie struggled. But it was no good. She was held fast. A hood was pulled over her head.

They looked at each other desperately. He had tried to fight back but it was hopeless.

His scream was cut off by a hand clamped across his mouth.

When she finally nodded that she would not scream for help, he removed his hand that had been clamped over her lips.

Suddenly, the cover was yanked away from her head. Blinking in the dazzling light, she tried to focus on the face looming above her.

One minute they were moving in single file along the side of the trail, and the next he was catapulted into the air by a large net. It had been covered by leaves and branches and attached to a tree.

For a moment, he hung there, swinging like a bag of coconuts.

It was dark outside and he wondered how long he had been held captive there. Where had they taken him?

Her first thought was to scream and shout and hammer on the door until someone came to let her out.

It was impossible to free or even loosen the bindings around her hands and feet.

She tried to wriggle her hands free of the ropes, but they were too tight. She slumped down, fighting back the tears.

The rope around his wrists was beginning to rub.

With her hands and feet bound, she shuffled over to the window, struggled to grasp the marble statue, and just managed to hold on to it. Her heart pounding, she inched her way to the door, shuffling and sliding on the wooden floor, raised the statue with all her strength, and waited for the door to open.

As the door closed, he slid down on his knees and slumped against the wall.

The door closed behind her, and locked. She was alone.

It was a cold night so they huddled together on the cold, concrete floor, sharing their warmth.

It was dark when he woke up. He was lying on his back and staring into blackness.

SECTION 3 – REACTION

WORDS

Nouns   **Misery**, grief, despair, loneliness, hopelessness

                        Heart, throat, lump, sobs

                        Face, mouth, jaw, chin, lips, teeth

                        Arms, shoulders, elbows, hand, fist, palms, knuckles, fingernails
                        Legs, knees, feet

                        Sigh, whisper, murmur, moan, groan, wail, howl

Adjectives   **Cold**, hollow

                        Painful, horrible

                        Sad, haunted

                        Wet, red, swollen, blotchy

                        Quiet, low, grave, solemn, husky, gruff, hoarse

                        Shaky, choking, quivering, shuddering

Verbs   **Filled**, welled, choked, broke, poured, spilled

                        Shook, trembled, wobbled

                        Twisted, tightened, faltered, crumpled

                        Bit, pressed, rubbed, jammed, chewed

                        Cried, sniffed, wept, sobbed

                        Cracked, swallowed, stifled, strangled

                        Wiped, brushed

                        Bent, stooped, hunched, slumped, slouched

                        Rocked, swayed, paced

PHRASES – NOUNS AND ADJECTIVES

★ Felt hollow and cold
★ Huge lump in the back of his throat
★ Horrible sense of loneliness and despair like a dark fog
★ All thought and reason had shut down
★ *Wet and red from weeping*
★ Swollen and blotchy

* Quivering lips
* Haunted expression
* Vacant expression
* As if in a trance
* *Quiet groan*
* Low, gurgling moan
* Moan of despair
* Stifled sob
* Silent, shuddering sobs
* Quivering whisper

PHRASES – VERBS

* Erupted inside him
* Enveloped her like a dark cloud
* Spread through his chest
* Washed over him
* Curled up and shrivelled
* Welled up in her throat
* Crushed his windpipe
* *Trembled as she spoke*
* Pressed her lips together
* Bit her lip until she drew blood
* Contorted with pain and misery
* *Streamed down her face*
* Spilled out of his eyes
* Blurred her vision
* Scalded her cheeks as they flowed
* Screwed her eyes shut to hold back the tears
* Stared unblinking at the door in front of him
* *Choked with misery*
* Swallowed hard before speaking
* Howled like a wounded dog
* *Pressed his palms into his eyes*
* Chewed her fingernails
* Bit her knuckles
* Jammed her knuckles against her teeth
* Brushed tears away with a clumsy fist
* Wiped his eyes with the back of his hand
* *Bent over with his elbows on his knees*
* Hugged her body with both arms
* Slumped like a puppet with its strings cut
* Rocked back and forth quietly

150 *Captured*

SENTENCES

The pain of his failure spread through his chest like a dull ache. He had been so close! There was no way he was going to be able to escape this time. With a moan of despair, he buried his head in his hands.

She felt a rush of misery surge into her chest and throat, and flood her eyes with tears.

He bit his lip to stem the tears that welled up in his eyes and threatened to spill onto his face.

Her face was shadowed with misery and regret, as she stared at the ground in front of her. How different things would have been if she had turned back.

When he spoke, his voice was a gruff whisper.

He held his body rigid – jaws tight, back hunched – elbows pressed into his knees.

Hugging her body with both arms, she swayed backwards and forwards.

Rubbing her eyes, she brushed away the tears that blurred her vision.

She closed her eyes. No more footsteps. Silence. Throbbing silence. All she could hear was her own heart thudding in her ears.

With a moan of despair, he slumped to the ground like a puppet with its strings cut.

Part 4
Survival

13

Fire, explosions, earthquakes and volcanoes

1. **Her mind was a fog of sheer panic** as the crackle of burning flames drifted towards her. Staggering to her feet, she made her way to the stairs, but as she turned the corner, **fear coursed through her veins**. A sea of flames ran swiftly along the ground like an orange tidal wave.

2. Spitting embers shot through the air; **her eyes snapped open in panic and swept over the scene of devastation in front of her**. Forced back by the flames, she had to crawl on all fours back down the corridor.

3. The windows were blown outwards, exploding into fragments and sending slithers of glass like lethal razor blades soaring through the air. As the ground trembled beneath her, she couldn't stay upright and was thrown violently backwards. **Curling herself up into a ball, shivering violently, she covered her head with her hands.**

4. The fountain of smoke choked and blinded her. **Hard to breathe, hard to see in the smoky, black haze, she couldn't make up her mind whether to go up or down.** She crouched low to the ground to duck under the smoke.

SECTION 1 – SETTING

A. Fire

WORDS	
Nouns	**Fire**, inferno, conflagration
	Flames, sparks, embers, cinders, shingles, glow
	Shower, streak, shafts, spout, arc, balls
	Column, sheet, wall
	Lava, steam
	Wind, breeze, gust
	City, rooftops, ground, corridor, passage, window, door, ceiling, beams
	Trees, branches, grass, morass
Similes/ Metaphors	**Rocket**, comet, tongues, fingers, wave, lake, sea
Adjectives	**Orange**, red, scarlet, glowing
	Roaring, rampaging, swirling, billowing, twisting
	Hot, searing, burning, blazing, fiery, flaring, crackling
	Ragged, manic
	Brief, fleeting, flickering
	Vast, dense
Verbs	**Burst**, sprang, flared, leapt, shot, soared, streaked, spouted, whirled, surged, darted
	Rose, floated, moved, licked, rippled, curled, slithered, flickered, skittered, rolled
	Fell, rained, descended
	Swept, surrounded, closed in, caught
	Glowed, glimmered
	Wrapped, chewed, burnt, scorched

PHRASES – NOUNS AND ADJECTIVES

- ★ Ragged wall of flames
- ★ Wave of fire
- ★ An inferno
- ★ Swirling churn of destruction
- ★ Rampaging, swirling, billowing flames
- ★ Blazing bedlam of fiery tongues
- ★ Balls of flame like comets
- ★ A twisting column of flame
- ★ Lake of fire
- ★ Vast sheet of flame
- ★ Sea of flames
- ★ Like torches in the hand of a destructive giant
- ★ *Shower of flaming, spitting embers*
- ★ Tongues of fire
- ★ Streak of orange flame
- ★ Flickering fires
- ★ Tongues of flame
- ★ Spouts of flame
- ★ Orange arc
- ★ Flaring, crackling flames
- ★ Burning branches
- ★ *Fingers of flame*
- ★ Fleeting tongue of orange
- ★ Flashes of orange
- ★ Brief spurt of flame
- ★ Red glow
- ★ Shafts of orange and scarlet
- ★ *Manic cinders*
- ★ Fiery shingles
- ★ Burning shingles
- ★ Searing, pulsating embers
- ★ Glowing light from the embers
- ★ *Blast of hot, crackling air*
- ★ Roaring wind
- ★ *Brilliant flash of light*
- ★ Blazing balls of lava
- ★ Dense forest of steam

PHRASES – VERBS

- ★ *Licked from the mouth of the passage*
- ★ Licked across the wooden beams
- ★ Fell in showers of sparks at her feet
- ★ Rippled in pools along the ground
- ★ Slithered through the grass
- ★ Moved through the trees
- ★ Flickered orange red
- ★ Cast flickering, jittery shadows
- ★ Flickered on and off
- ★ Sprang out of the ground
- ★ *Burst up and out of . . .*
- ★ Whirled and skittered into the sky
- ★ Sent sparks skyward in a manic rush
- ★ Sent embers flying
- ★ Leapt erratically in the wind
- ★ Surged rapidly up and along the roof
- ★ Darted through the air
- ★ Shot into the air like a rocket
- ★ Caught in a fiery, devilish dancing whirlwind
- ★ Spouted high in the air
- ★ Shot through the air
- ★ Soared upwards to light up the sky
- ★ Flared to life in all directions
- ★ Darted through the open doors
- ★ *Rained down*
- ★ Streaked down
- ★ Ran swiftly along the ground
- ★ Descended about them in a rain of sparks
- ★ Rolled down on them in billows and sheets
- ★ *Swept over her*
- ★ Surrounded by . . .
- ★ Closing in on either side
- ★ Caught in the conflagration
- ★ *Burned everywhere*
- ★ Disappeared in flames and darkness
- ★ Glimmered briefly as the city burned
- ★ *Curled out of all the windows*
- ★ Floated from the roof
- ★ Appeared above the rooftops
- ★ Caught in the branches of the trees
- ★ Curled down the ceiling
- ★ Burst up from the morass

* Rose to engulf the room
* *Chewed through the wood*
* Wrapped around the wood

SENTENCES

A wave of fire surged rapidly up and along the roof.

The fire had grown to an inferno and was surging from house to house.

The city was a blazing bedlam with rampaging, swirling tongues of fire that flared to life in all directions.

A shower of flaming, spitting embers shot through the air.

The passage was a sea of flames that ran swiftly along the ground like an orange tidal wave.

The flaring, crackling flames shot into the air like a rocket, scorched the ceiling and then licked and spat across the wooden beams.

Raining down on them in billows and sheets, the balls of flames were like fiery comets that plummeted to the ground and wrapped themselves around the wood, the trees, the branches.

A streak of orange flame slithered through the grass.

B. Explosions

WORDS

Nouns	**Crash**, explosion, detonations, burning
	Sirens, alarms, screams, shrieks, howl, roar
	Crackle, sizzle, groan, crack
	Building, roof, walls, windows
	Metal, wood, timbers, glass, rubber, petrol
	Debris, fragments
	Avalanche, stampede
Similes/ Metaphors	**Razor blades**, giant snakes, train in a tunnel
Adjectives	**Thunderous**, exploding, crashing, roaring, shrieking, howling, whining

Ear-splitting, ear-rending, ear-piercing

Grating, grinding, splintering, tearing, twisting

Dull, muffled

Blaring, flashing

Verbs   **Heard**, drifted, echoed, pierced

Filled, pounded, thudded, battered, deafened

Shuddered, shifted, rumbled, shook, tilted, shattered, erupted, exploded, crashed, collapsed

Whistled, hissed, crackled, tinkled, crunched

Hurtled, ripped, surged, cascaded

Showered, spluttered, bounced, ricocheted

PHRASES – NOUNS AND ADJECTIVES

- ★ *From the street below*
- ★ From deep beneath the ground
- ★ Another crash outside
- ★ Thunderous crash overhead
- ★ *Crash and crackle of burning*
- ★ Crackle of dry bush
- ★ Angry sizzle
- ★ Crackling roar
- ★ Crackling, roaring reeds
- ★ Hissing and crackling . . . distant screams and shrieks
- ★ Crackling and popping sounds
- ★ *Dull clang of metal collapsing*
- ★ Shriek of tearing metal
- ★ Tearing noise
- ★ Deep howl of twisting metal
- ★ Mechanical screeching
- ★ *Cascade of detonations*
- ★ Shock waves
- ★ *Sound of shattering glass*
- ★ Icicles of glass
- ★ Shards of glass
- ★ Slithers of glass like lethal transparent razor blades
- ★ *Blaring sirens, flashing lights*
- ★ Whining scream
- ★ *Grating, grinding roar*
- ★ Shrieking fire

- Ear-piercing whistle
- Ear-splitting roar
- Ear-rending splinter of wood
- Brutal grating sound
- Groan and a crack behind them
- Thunderous roar
- Deep, splintering scream
- *Massive explosion*
- Muffled boom like the sound of a train approaching in a tunnel
- Like a score of giants were stamping their feet
- Exploding windows, crashing beams
- An avalanche of timbers

PHRASES – VERBS

- Heard the glass shatter
- Exploded into fragments
- Showered them
- Crackled and tinkled as the windows collapsed
- Crunched pieces of glass beneath her feet
- *Whistled across the room*
- Spluttered in the wind
- Hissed like a chorus of snakes
- *Echoed up from the bowels of the building*
- Pierced the air
- Drifted to them on the wind
- *Filled her ears*
- Throbbed in her ears
- Pounded her ears
- Battered her ears
- Deafened him
- Swallowed up by the noise
- Thudded against her chest
- *Shuddered in their frames*
- Shifted and rumbled beneath him
- Tilted wildly
- Shook the building
- Ripped through the building
- Shook for a moment then collapsed
- Began to ripple and fold
- Gave way and collapsed
- Crashed to the ground
- *Exploded across the room*
- Cascaded from the roof

★ Exploded into a myriad of fragments
★ Shattered into hundreds of tiny glass pebbles
★ Erupted around him
★ Bounced around the room
★ Ricocheted off the walls
★ Surged into the room
★ *Filled with the stench of burning rubber and petrol*

SENTENCES

From deep beneath the ground, there was a thunderous roar, which made the windows shudder in their frames and the furniture tilt wildly.

The crash and crackle of burning drifted towards them, and then a sound like a roaring wind filled their ears as the explosion surged towards them.

The windows were blown outwards, exploding into fragments and sending slithers of glass like lethal razor blades soaring to the ground.

There was nothing left of the door but a few burnt, scorched fragments swinging on their hinges.

There was a dull clang and then a shriek of tearing metal as the building buckled.

The explosion ripped through the building, battering her ears and thudding against her chest.

The floor shifted and rumbled beneath him, and then the door was torn from its hinges and exploded into fragments.

The ground bucked away beneath them and then fell away. A bank of mud was heaved up from the massive crack in the earth.

A tidal wave of mud and trees and branches ploughed towards him. He didn't even have time to shout.

C. Earthquakes and volcanoes

WORDS

Nouns	**Ground**, earth, crater, fountain, cauldron
	Clouds, steam, bubbles, fumes, fire, smoke, gases, ash, rocks, lava, mud
	Horizon, haze, hell
	Stench, reek, fumes, sulphur

Adjectives	**Silent**, menacing
	Smoky, black, choking, white-hot
	Spitting, hissing, belching, smouldering
	Throbbing, thudding, deafening
	Poisonous
Verbs	**Shook**, trembled, exploded, erupted
	Bubbled, spat, hissed, boomed, roared
	Crashed, rained

PHRASES – NOUNS AND ADJECTIVES

- ⭐ White-hot steam
- ⭐ Choking fumes
- ⭐ Fountain of fire like a throbbing wound
- ⭐ Huge, black clouds
- ⭐ Towering, black clouds of ash and smoke
- ⭐ *Smouldering ash and rocks*
- ⭐ Cloud of dust and debris
- ⭐ Poisonous gases and ash
- ⭐ Cauldron of spitting bubbles, hissing steam and belching fumes
- ⭐ Vision of hell

PHRASES – VERBS

- ⭐ Hung ominously over the town
- ⭐ *Trembled and shook*
- ⭐ Rumbled and trembled
- ⭐ *Erupted out of the crater*
- ⭐ Spread outwards
- ⭐ *Blocked out the sun and darkness fell*
- ⭐ Swallowed the horizon
- ⭐ Swallowed up the light
- ⭐ *Rained from the sky*
- ⭐ Poured down
- ⭐ Spat poisonous gases and ash into the air
- ⭐ *Stank of sulphur*
- ⭐ *Followed by a deafening boom*
- ⭐ Turned the town into a vision of hell

SENTENCES

The earth trembled and shook, sending everything crashing to the ground in a cloud of dust and debris.

The earth rumbled and trembled as if an angry giant was marching nearer, stamping his feet, shaking the ground with every step.

It was as if the ground itself was writhing and bucking in an underground storm.

The air was thick with choking fumes. It was hard to breathe and hard to see in the smoky, black haze.

Huge, black clouds blocked out the sun, and darkness fell.

Torrents of sizzling, smouldering ash and rocks rained from the sky.

As the volcano erupted, the ground trembled and shook, followed by a deafening boom as a fountain of fire, like a throbbing wound, flooded the sky.

SECTION 2 – INTERACTION

WORDS

Nouns	**Ground**, crack, split, chasm
	Landslide, mud, trees, branches, debris
	Blast, explosion, fire, flames, smoke, embers, fumes
	Atmosphere, haze
	Street, crowds, passage, corridor, stairs, banister, rail, window, sill, door, drainpipe
	Lungs, breath, mouth, nose, eyes, head, arms, fingers, legs, feet, shoulder, back, skin
Adjectives	**Hot**, burning, scorching, searing
	Thick, dense, towering, jagged, gnarled
	Choking, poisonous
Verbs	**Made for**, headed towards
	Darted, leapt, lunged, climbed, dropped
	Ducked, crouched, scrambled, staggered, forced back, fought
	Fell, thrown, knocked, stumbled, tumbled, pitched

Rolled, slid, clung, clawed

Spotted, searched, scanned, peered

Covered, held up, sucked, gasped, coughed

Burned, scorched

Grabbed, draped, dragged, hauled, hurled

Moaned, groaned

Filled, blew, drowned

PHRASES – NOUNS AND ADJECTIVES

- Once on the ground floor
- One step at a time
- *Jagged crack in the concrete*
- Towering wall of fire
- Blast of heat
- Scorching metal
- Crackle of burning wood
- *Finger of smoke down her throat*
- Poisonous atmosphere
- Thick haze
- Choking fumes
- *Difficult to see*
- Watering eyes
- *Injured leg*
- *Screaming crowds, stampeding feet*

PHRASES – VERBS

- *Time was running out*
- No turning back now
- *Made for the stairs*
- Darted towards the window
- Forced back by the flames
- *Drowning in a sea of fire*
- Filled with the crackle of burning wood
- Blew like a bellows, fanning the flames
- *Crouched low to the ground*
- Ducked under the smoke
- Fought his way through the flames
- Leapt over a jagged crack

* Staggered, ran, fought their way through ...
* Staggered to her feet
* Staggered along the passage
* Tried to run away
* Tried to walk
* Felt their way
* *Couldn't stay upright*
* Thrown off his feet
* Thrown onto his back
* Knocked backwards by the force of the blast
* Half fell down the rest of the stairs
* Scrambled forwards on all fours
* *Rolled helplessly*
* Clawed at the ground to stop herself toppling into the chasm
* Pitched through empty space
* *Covered his mouth and nose*
* Threw his arm across his eyes
* Held up her hands to shield her face from the heat
* Forced himself to suck in hot air
* Sucked all the air out of his lungs
* Gasped for breath
* Scorched his lungs
* Coughed and gasped
* Felt a wave of searing, scalding heat
* Felt as if she was inhaling flames
* *Brushed off a burning ember*
* Burned through her fingers
* Scorched her skin
* *Grabbed her arm*
* Draped her arm around her shoulder
* Dragged the two of them out onto the street
* Hauled her away from the surging blast
* Scrambled over to help him up
* *Looked around, bewildered*
* Didn't know whether to go up or down
* Moaned and tried to move her head
* Placed a hand on the banister to steady herself
* *Threw himself towards the door*
* Lunged closer to the flames
* Spotted a small window
* Searched desperately for a rope
* Grabbed a chair
* Smashed the window
* Climbed onto the sill

- ☆ Peered down
- ☆ Searched the wall for a drainpipe
- ☆ Slid out through the window
- ☆ *Tumbled down helplessly in a landslide*
- ☆ Showered him, filled his mouth, got in his eyes
- ☆ *Ran for the nearest tree*
- ☆ Grabbed for the thick, gnarled branches
- ☆ Tried to haul himself out of range
- ☆ Hurled himself clear
- ☆ Clung to a tree
- ☆ Managed to hold on
- ☆ Dropped down
- ☆ *Shaken so hard his teeth rattled*

SENTENCES

He crouched low to the ground to duck under the smoke.

She stumbled and flung her hand out in front of her, groping for something to stop her falling.

He slithered to a halt and stood with his hands on hips, head bowed, gasping for breath.

Staggering to her feet, she made her way to the stairs, but the landing was filled with the crackle of burning flames. Forced back by the flames, she had to crawl on all fours back down the corridor.

Grabbing a chair, she smashed the window, climbed out onto the sill and stretched out her arm to grab the drainpipe. Wrapping her arms and legs round the pipe, she gradually inched her way down to the ground.

She held up her hands to shield her face from the heat, but it was no good, a blast of searing heat burned through her fingers and sucked all the air out of her lungs.

He draped his arm around Kitty, who groaned as she tried to put weight on her leg. He looked round and saw that the first floor was already engulfed in a towering wall of flame. There was no turning back now. Taking her full weight, they staggered down the stairs, stumbling down to the ground floor.

He was knocked backwards by the force of the blast. It was like the ground itself was writhing and bucking in an underground storm. He couldn't stay upright. He was thrown violently backwards.

Suddenly, he was tumbling head over heels in a landslide, drowning in a tidal wave of mud and trees and branches, that cascaded down onto his head and filled his mouth. Desperately, he clawed at the ground to stop himself toppling into the chasm that had opened up in front of him.

SECTION 3 – REACTION

WORDS

Nouns	**Terror**, panic
	Heart, pulse, chest, ribs
	Hands, head, teeth, eyes
	Movement
Adjectives	**Urgent**, desperate
	Shallow, deep
	Wide, staring
	Dizzy, disoriented
Verbs	**Snaked**, squeezed, jolted, surged, blasted, flooded, hammered
	Trembled, shook, shivered, rattled
	Flung, threw, curled
	Prayed, winced, yelled, screamed, howled
	Stood, rooted, paralysed
	Blinded

PHRASES – NOUNS AND ADJECTIVES

- ★ Once on the ground floor . . .
- ★ No turning back now
- ★ 'Move or die'
- ★ *Head was swimming*
- ★ Completely disoriented
- ★ *Face urgent and twisted with terror and panic*
- ★ Wide, staring eyes
- ★ *Every movement an effort*
- ★ Desperate yell for help

PHRASES – VERBS

- ★ Had only minutes to break out
- ★ Couldn't make his mind up whether to go up or down
- ★ Saw how high up he was
- ★ *Squeezed her heart*

* Flooded through his veins
* *Screamed at him to...*
* Jolted her out of her paralysis
* Developed a life of its own as if fuelled by the lethal fumes
* Snaked around his windpipe
* Choked his breath into shallow gasps
* Blasted by an explosion of terror
* Shrivelled with fear
* Surged through her
* Made her wince and tremble
* Hammered against her ribs
* *Unable to breathe*
* Fought to breathe
* Drew in a deep breath
* Fought for air
* Choked his breath
* Choked and blinded her until it passed
* *Threw himself towards the door*
* *Snapped open in panic*
* Swept over the scene of devastation in front of him
* *Stood rooted to the spot*
* Paralysed by fear, as if turned to stone
* *Edged with panic*
* Prayed that it was open
* Blew out hard to stop herself howling
* Whispered as they crackled and sputtered around him
* Flung her head back and shrieked
* Screamed as the tree that he was holding onto started to uproot
* *Curled herself into a ball*
* Shivered violently
* Covered her head with her hands
* Shaken so hard his teeth rattled

SENTENCES

He had only minutes to break out. Very soon he would be unable to breathe.

The sound of the deafening explosion jolted her out of her paralysis.

'Move or die', whispered the flames, as they crackled and sputtered around him.

He tumbled down the slope and was shaken so hard his teeth rattled.

She screamed as the tree that she was holding onto started to uproot. She started to slide again.

There was no turning back now. His voice was edged with panic, but he gritted his teeth and stumbled forward.

Terror squeezed her heart as she stared at the roaring flames in front of her.

Fear was flooding through her veins. Her mind was a fog of sheer panic.

He threw himself towards the door, praying that it was open.

His heart shrivelled with fear when he looked out of the window and saw how high up he was.

His head was swimming. He was completely disoriented. He couldn't make his mind up whether to go up or down.

Every movement was an effort, fighting to breathe, forcing himself to keep moving.

The fountain of smoke choked and blinded her until it passed. She bent over, hands on her knees, her lungs fighting for air.

All his instincts screamed at him to get to the sea before the tidal wave of lava descended on the village.

Fear developed a life of its own as if fuelled by the lethal fumes.

Panic snaked around his windpipe and choked his breath into shallow gasps.

Drawing in a deep breath, she blew it out hard to stop herself howling and force herself to keep calm . . . keep moving.

She was blasted by an explosion of terror that surged through her and made her wince and tremble, her heart hammering against her ribs.

His wide, staring eyes were filled with dread. His face was urgent and twisted with terror and panic.

His eyes snapped open in panic and swept over the scene of devastation in front of him. Horror gripped him like a snake coiling around his windpipe and choked his breath.

The silence of the forest was ripped apart by a sound like a roaring, fiery wind. She stood rooted to the spot, paralysed by fear, as if turned to stone.

She flung her head back and screamed – a desperate yell for help!

She curled herself into a ball, shivering violently and covered her head with her hands.

14

In the water

1. A dark mass on the horizon . . . a huge wave a long way off, but getting bigger and bigger and moving very fast towards them.

   He was horror-struck. It was like nothing he had ever seen before. It was massive, hideous, unstoppable. **He stared unblinking, as if in a trance.** There was no way to avoid it. It was heading straight for them.

   It was as if time had stopped. **He stood perfectly still, frozen to the deck, gripping the rail, paralysed by fear.**

2. He was falling, plummeting towards the water. As he descended, a huge blanket of water crashed down on him. He hit the sea and went under.

   Sucked inside, dragged down, he was swept along by the ferocious current, tumbling head over heels in the churning water.

   Just for a moment, the water released him and he rose to the surface. **Spluttering and choking, he sucked in air, coughing violently.** He had barely caught his breath before he was slammed in the back by another wave and submerged again. **This one drained what little strength he had left. He had reached his limit. He couldn't go on.**

3. The river was wide and fast-flowing, too deep to wade, but a dangerous place to swim, the bend in the river beckoning like a bony finger of death. If he was spotted halfway across he would be an easy target, but he had no choice but to attempt to cross it. He knew he would have to swim most of the way under-water, and **he prayed he would have enough strength to keep beneath the surface until he was beyond the bend**.

   He took a deep breath, filling his lungs, and slipped under the surface, plunging his head beneath the icy water until he was completely submerged.

SECTION 1 – SETTING

WORDS

Nouns
Slopes, banks

Cliffs, rock-face, rocks, boulders

Depth, current, rapids, waterfall, fountain

Wave, spray, mist, foam

Trunks, branches, willows, driftwood, seaweed, plants, weeds, reeds

Seagulls, curlews, heron, geese

Adjectives
Brown, grey, dark, gloomy, black, inky, misty, eerie

Greasy, oily, murky

Swollen, stormy, bulging, restless, boiling, foaming, churning, frothing, swirling, seething, flying

Wild, raging, roaring, thunderous, pounding, relentless

Deadly, savage, ominous, threatening, menacing, monstrous, treacherous

Deep

Cold, chilly, icy, freezing

Rotting, decaying, drooping

Sharp, rough, jagged

Verbs
Swelled, soared, surged

Battered, hammered, pounded, blasted, shredded

Rushed, sped, swept, gushed, burst, flooded, showered, crashed, hurtled, plunged, cascaded, rampaged

Rose, reared, jutted, littered

Lurched, hurled, capsized

Raged, roared, thundered

PHRASES – NOUNS AND ADJECTIVES

★ At the mercy of the wind and waves
★ No sign or sound of a human

* *Under the cloak of darkness*
* Onset of darkness
* *Within a short distance of them*
* Away to the east
* Beyond the bend in the headland
* *Closer and closer*
* Nearer and nearer to the shore
* *Dark, cold water of the sea far below*
* Black world of the deep, restless ocean
* Bulging blister of churning, grey water
* Black blanket of swirling sea and stormy sky
* Too deep to wade and too dangerous to swim
* *Dark mass on the horizon*
* Big wave a long way off
* Massive waves
* Monstrous eight-metre waves
* Mountain of water
* Torrent of water
* Seething black wall of water
* Massive, menacing, unstoppable wave of water
* *Massive crest of churning foam*
* Churning surface of the waves
* Ribbon of white surf
* Crest of swirling, white spray
* Boiling, flying foam
* Huge clouds of spray
* *Wild current*
* Watery grave
* *Top of the falls*
* Ten-metre-high waterfall
* Sheer drop to the water below
* Misty void below
* At the bottom of the steep falls
* Boiling mass of rapids
* Relentless stream of water
* Boiling, foaming cauldron
* Like a seething cauldron
* Churning white water
* Icy mist
* Fountains of white spray
* White, swirling foam
* *Dense bank of reeds*
* Rotting plants
* Drooping willows

* *Jagged rocks*
* Stones as sharp as knives
* Jagged and deadly
* Like fins of circling sharks
* *Savage range of rocks*
* Sheer rock-face
* Treacherous, unyielding outcrop of rocks
* Crags of rock like fangs
* *Scattering of driftwood and seaweed*
* Peppering of driftwood
* Trunks as big as telephone poles
* *Huge fragments of ice as big as islands*
* As deadly as solid rock
* *Inky depths*
* Eerie, green, underwater forest
* Eerie world of dark, green water
* Spidery web of weeds
* *Quiet, too quiet*
* Faint roar across the horizon
* Warning groan and rumble of the huge wave
* *Rushing, roaring sound of the water*
* Like a screaming jet engine
* Pounding roar
* Booming breakers
* A snarling monster
* Deafening roar like thunder
* Deadly sound of roaring rapids
* *Large flock of shrieking seagulls*
* Sudden screech of a heron
* Sudden squawking of geese
* Cry of curlews
* *Hissing foam*
* Whooshing whirlpool of bubbles and water
* Constant thud and swish of the waves against the hull
* *Creak of oars against the side of the boat*

PHRASES – VERBS

* Rose higher and higher
* Rose in a huge arch above the boat
* Getting bigger
* Soared high in the air
* *Moving very fast*
* Thundered nearer and nearer to the shore

- Rushed and roared, surged and soared
- Threatened to bury them in a watery grave
- *Battered the ship*
- Broke against the sides of the boat
- *Crashed onto the rocks*
- Rampaged down the rocks
- Hammered the shore
- Hurtled over every barrier in its path
- Shredded by the rocks
- *Crashed down on them*
- Caught in a current
- Raged around her
- Boiled around her ankles
- Rushed past like a surging torrent
- Pummelled and tossed by the brutal power of the waves
- *Crashed far below*
- Roared over the reef
- Boiled around the rocks
- Hurtled over the edge into the misty void below
- Plunged down the cliffs
- Cascaded over the top of the falls
- *Reared a savage range of rocks*
- Jutted from the river
- Rose up from the water ahead of him
- Driven perilously close to them
- Threatened to smash them against the rocks
- Hurled against the rocks
- Hurtled past, exposing their huge balls of roots
- Reached out for the raft
- Crashed through the rocks
- *Arrowed down the river*
- Lurched as a second wave pounded it
- Capsized the craft
- *Overhung a small bank at the side of the river*
- Choked the shallows at the water's edge
- *Licked up to her knees*
- Showered them all with the icy seawater

SENTENCES

She had dived into an eerie world; an underwater forest of murky, green water, strangled by a spidery web of weeds and coated with scum. It smelt revolting. She could barely see a few centimetres into its gloomy depths.

The wild current swept past and flung the water into the air as it tumbled over the edge.

The waterfall rampaged down the rocks and blanketed everything with its pounding roar. There was a sheer drop to the water below. At the bottom of the falls was a seething cauldron of churning white water.

The current was shredded by the rocks, thrusting through like the teeth of an enormous comb and churning the water into a tumult of flying foam.

They were at the mercy of the wind and waves. Ahead and below them it was dark. They were trapped by the black blanket of the deep, swirling sea and stormy sky.

He was caught in the seething cauldron, which tugged at him, sucked him into its swirling surface and dragged him into its inky depths.

They could see a dark mass on the horizon ... huge waves a long way off, but getting bigger and bigger and moving very fast towards them. It was like nothing he had ever seen before. It was massive, hideous, unstoppable. It was heading right for them. There was no way around it.

The wave rose higher and higher; thundered nearer and nearer; rose in an arch high above the boat, and then broke into a roar of boiling foam, which swirled and seethed around the boat, pummelling and tossing it with its brutal power, threatening to bury them in a watery grave.

As darkness fell, the storm worsened. The waves battered the ship, breaking against its sides and showering them all with icy seawater.

Roaring towards them were monstrous eight-metre-high waves. Ahead, a savage range of rocks as sharp as knives, reared up out of the water. They held their breath as they were driven perilously close to them, every violent gust and heave of water threatening to smash them against the treacherous rocks.

The shriek of a seagull broke the eerie silence and they looked up to see a large flock circling the boat.

The river was wide and fast-flowing, too deep to wade, but a dangerous place to swim, the bend in the river beckoning like a bony finger of death. If he was spotted halfway across he would be an easy target, but he had no choice but to attempt to cross it.

The river had become a surging torrent; a bulging blister of churning, grey water. It had torn whole trees out of the ground, and swept them away. Trunks as big as telephone poles hurtled past, their root balls exposed, their branches reaching out to grab the raft and drag it along with them.

Below him, everything seemed jagged and deadly. Huge crags of rock jutted from the river like fangs, turning the water into a boiling mass of rapids.

SECTION 2 – INTERACTION

WORDS

Nouns

Ocean, sea, river, rapids, waterfalls, waves

Surface, shallows, edge, bottom, riverbed

Current, whirlpool, cauldron

Shore, beach, headland, riverbank

Rocks, boulders, pothole, mud

Footing, steps, grip, purchase, balance, strokes

Head, neck, mouth, chest, waist, belly, back, shoulder, legs, arms, hand, fingers

Air, breath, lungs, gasps

Raft, boat, canoe

Log, rope, lifebelt

Adjectives

Soft, muddy, slimy, sandy

Rocky, jagged, deadly, vicious

Low, deep, shallow

Frantic, desperate, weak

Huge, massive

Verbs

Thought, realised, urged, impelled

Stepped, plodded, waded

Slipped, stumbled, slithered

Crouched, lowered, sunk

Jumped, dived, ducked, launched, plunged, hurtled, plummeted

Hit, smashed, smacked, slammed, slapped, crushed, pounded

Wrapped, locked, trapped

Cut, sliced, tore, ripped

Dragged down, pulled, tugged, sucked inside, swept, spun, twisted

Dumped, submerged, disappeared, vanished

Swam, kicked, pumped, thrashed, struggled, flailed, floundered, scrabbled

Belly-crawled, treaded

Held, extended, clawed, clung, grabbed, grasped, pulled, hauled

Missed, avoided, dodged

Brushed, touched, reached

Broke, rose, ascended

Staggered, collapsed

Saw, filtered down, searched

Gulped, sucked, inhaled, dribbled, exhaled

Coughed, spluttered, squeezed

PHRASES – NOUNS AND ADJECTIVES

* *Not enough time to . . .*
* Next minute was the longest of his life
* All of a sudden
* Another couple of steps
* With all his strength
* Faster and faster
* *Up to his chest*
* Waist level
* Over her head
* *Parallel to the shore*
* Towards the rocks
* Diagonally back to the beach
* *Darkness and silence*
* Low rumble
* *Icy water like a vice around his chest*
* Icy embrace of the water
* *Sandy bottom*
* Sticking, muddy embrace
* Jagged shore
* Rocky edge

PHRASES – VERBS

* Realised too late
* Could not beat the pull of the ocean
* Didn't think he was going to be able to stop before the rapids

- ★ Couldn't tell which way was up and which way was down
- ★ Realised he wasn't getting anywhere
- ★ Impelled her to keep swimming
- ★ *Took a few steps to the riverbank*
- ★ Plodded through the soft mud
- ★ Waded slowly
- ★ Waded down the slope until the water was up to his chest
- ★ *Lost his footing*
- ★ Slipped, fell, hit the water
- ★ Stumbled into a pothole and overbalanced
- ★ Slithered in the mud
- ★ *Slipped into the water*
- ★ Crouched low in the water
- ★ Slithered back into the river
- ★ Lowered herself onto her belly
- ★ Pulled herself deeper
- ★ Sunk to her neck
- ★ *Jumped and barely cleared the rocks below*
- ★ Dived down into the water
- ★ *Slipped under the water*
- ★ Plunged her head beneath the icy water
- ★ Dived deep and swam for the side of . . .
- ★ Dived beneath the surface
- ★ Paddled himself under again
- ★ Plunged into the sea
- ★ Launched himself off the side
- ★ Plummeted towards the water
- ★ *Hung in space*
- ★ Falling, half in the water, half in the air
- ★ Hit the cauldron of water
- ★ Sucked inside and dragged down
- ★ Felt his legs and stomach take the full impact
- ★ Pounded down on his shoulders
- ★ Crushed him
- ★ Dragged him into its inky depths
- ★ Trapped his legs
- ★ Couldn't pull them free
- ★ *Floundered, scrabbled desperately with his hands*
- ★ Tried to free himself from the boat
- ★ Twisted his lower body
- ★ Missed a vicious black boulder by millimetres
- ★ *Sucked into the whirlpool*
- ★ Hurtled downwards into the darkness
- ★ *Threw himself sideways*

* Turned head-over-heels
* Waved her arms in circles
* *Treaded water for a moment*
* Stayed afloat by tilting his head back so that his mouth stayed in the air
* *Extended a hand over his head*
* Held each other up when they were knocked off balance
* Floundered, with his hands thrashing above his head
* *Ducked under the swirling wave*
* Thrashed in the water
* Half-waded, half-swam
* Put his head down
* Swam a few frantic strokes
* Kicked furiously
* Kicked his legs, pumped his arms, swam for his life
* Fought desperately against the current
* Swam hard for the rocks
* *Struggled weakly*
* Struggled desperately to stay afloat
* *Dragged her under*
* Swept along by the current
* Submerged completely
* Spun her around
* Dumped her on her back
* Sideswiped by a massive wave
* Tugged and pulled at his legs
* Smashed onto his head
* Crushed him from all sides
* Slammed against her back
* Surged around her legs
* *Disappeared beneath the surface*
* Couldn't find the bottom
* Made contact with the riverbed
* Brushed the sandy bottom
* Touched a toe on the bottom
* *Regained his balance*
* Scrambled for purchase
* Found a grip
* *Saw only the faintest glimmer of light*
* Filtered down through the murky river
* Grew slowly closer
* *Stayed down as long as her lungs could stand it*
* Swam underwater until she reached the bank
* Belly-crawled up from the water
* *Tried to fight his way to the surface*

* Pushed herself upwards
* Kept herself from floating too quickly to the surface by . . .
* *Broke the surface*
* Came up, gasping
* *Clung to the rock*
* Clawed at the water until her fingers found . . .
* Flailed around, searching for something solid
* Ascended slowly until his fingers touched . . .
* Groped about like a blind man
* Rose and grasped a knob of rock
* Grabbed hold of the log
* Grabbed hold of the lifebelt
* Grabbed hold of the slimy rope
* Saved him from being swept away
* *Pulled herself up into the shallows*
* Staggered up the bank, collapsed, panting
* Hauled herself over the side
* Collapsed onto his makeshift raft
* Lay in the shadow of the rocks where he could not be seen
* *Came up for air*
* Fought for air
* Took several deep breaths
* Gulped a few breaths
* Sucked in air
* Inhaled until his lungs were full
* Managed only shallow gasps
* Dribbled air from his mouth
* Exhaled as he rose
* Forced the breath from her lungs
* Squeezed her chest
* Coughed and spluttered
* *Smacked against his face*
* Slapped in the face by a huge wave
* Sliced at her face like a knife
* Cut through her flesh and straight into her bones
* Wrapped its chill around her
* Locked every muscle tight
* Couldn't see; couldn't breathe
* *Forced her eyes open*
* Opened his eyes to find . . .
* *Listened for any sound*
* Could hear the water thundering down
* Drowned out every other sound
* Reduced to a low rumble

SENTENCES

She hit the water, hurtled downwards into darkness and silence, turning head-over-heels until she did not know which way was up and which was down.

He took a deep breath, filling his lungs, and slipped under the water, plunging his head beneath the icy water until he was completely submerged.

Katie took one quick look and then jumped, barely clearing the rocks below as she plummeted towards the water.

The churning, icy water dragged her down; the current tugging and pulling at her legs; the waves smashing onto her head and slamming against her back.

As he was pulled under the water, Tom floundered, his hands thrashing above his head. Suddenly, his foot made contact with the riverbed and he pushed himself upwards, clawing at the water until his fingers found the outstretched limb of a tree that had been uprooted in the storm.

She dug deep and with every ounce of strength she possessed, kicked furiously for the shore.

He realised he wasn't getting anywhere. He was fighting against the current. A wave smacked against his face and he was submerged again.

She waved her arms in circles to keep herself from floating too quickly to the surface, staying down as long as her lungs could stand it, not daring to rise to the surface too near the riverbank.

He was falling, half in the water, and half in the air. As he descended, a huge blanket of water fell on him. He hit the water and went under. Sucked inside, dragged down, he began to move swiftly, swept along by the ferocious current.

The faintest glimmer of light filtered down through the murky water. She kicked furiously and with a few powerful strokes, broke the surface of the water, gasping for breath.

He flailed around, searching for something solid, groping around like a blind man. As he was about to give up hope, his hand grabbed hold of the slimy rope.

She hauled herself over the side and lay on the deck, her body racked by shallow, shuddering breaths.

He pulled himself up into the shallows, and lay in the shadow of the rocks where he could not be seen.

The next minute was the longest of his life. Curling his head into his body, he pushed with the paddle, rolled his hips and tried to turn the canoe over. His legs were trapped. Desperately, he twisted his lower body, trying to free his legs.

SECTION 3 – REACTION

WORDS

Nouns	**Time**, moment
	Sense, mind, brain, feeling, exhaustion, shivers
	Strength, muscles, rhythm
	Limbs, arms, legs, fingers, toes
	Head, eyelids, heart, voice, breath, air
	Calm, panic
Similes/ Metaphors	**Wood**, lead, claws, drum
Adjectives	**Deep**, shuddering, shivering, convulsing
	Heavy, limp, numb, aching, burning
Verbs	**Inhaled**, exhaled, sucked, gasped, sputtered, spluttered, coughed, racked
	Pounded, pummelled, burnt
	Drained, numbed, paralysed
	Froze, choked, stripped away
	Crept, felt, thought
	Rolled, hugged, dangled

PHRASES – NOUNS AND ADJECTIVES

- ★ No time to think, no time to do anything
- ★ At the very last moment
- ★ With every ounce of strength
- ★ Light-headed with exhaustion
- ★ Like pieces of wood

PHRASES – VERBS

- ★ Took a deep, shuddering breath
- ★ Screamed for air
- ★ Inhaled deeply

- Gasping and coughing
- Sucked in air, and coughed violently
- Gasped and sputtered
- Coughed and spluttered
- *Turned her hands into shivering claws*
- Gnawed at his fingers and toes
- Racked with convulsing shivers
- *Paralysed every muscle*
- Exhausted body felt full of lead
- Grew as heavy as lead
- Started to lose rhythm
- Drained what little strength he had left
- Felt heavy and impossible to lift
- Dangled limply in the water
- Felt battered and bruised, utterly exhausted
- Pummelled into burning knots
- Lost all memory of how to move her numb limbs
- *Tried to remain calm*
- Dug deep
- *Froze her heart, trapping her voice*
- Choked by an invisible hand
- Stripped away any sense of up and down
- Crept into his mind
- Had gone blank
- Felt as if his brain was being squeezed
- Beginning to set in
- Unable to see or feel anything
- Thought he was trapped in a watery grave
- *Hugged herself with her arms*
- Rolled into a ball
- *Head pounded, eyelids burnt*
- Pounded like a drum
- Looked wildly around

SENTENCES

The icy water had turned her hands into shivering claws.

A weary numbness was creeping into her arms and legs.

He prayed he would have enough strength to swim back to the boat.

He was slammed in the back by another wave, which drained what little strength he had left, and submerged him again, sending despairing thoughts racing through his head that he would end up being trapped in a watery grave.

She was starting to lose all memory of how to move her numb limbs. Her heart pounded like a drum, and panic was beginning to set in.

She felt as if her brain was being squeezed. Her mind had gone blank. She was unable to see or feel anything. The cold had gnawed at her fingers and toes, frozen her mind.

She felt battered and bruised, utterly exhausted. The seething, swirling surf had frozen her heart, trapped her voice. It was as if she had been choked by an invisible hand that had racked her body with convulsing shivers. Her arms dangled limply in the water. They felt heavy and impossible to lift.

He heaved air into his strained lungs.

He had reached his limit. He couldn't go on. His body was rebelling, shutting down. His muscles ached with the sickening pain. It was as if someone had sprinkled red-hot needles across his legs and arms.

Every second the pain was getting worse. She couldn't carry on for much longer. Her head began to pound, her lungs to squeeze tight and her brain to spin wildly. Now all she could hear was the ringing in her ears as she started to black out.

15
Deserts

THE S/C-I-R STRUCTURE

1. They made painfully slow progress, little more than a shuffle that kicked the sand and dust into the air and filled their eyes, their noses, their ears, their mouths.

   The desert was a burning, merciless furnace of glare and death, and bleached skeletons of dead men who had been lost in the great ocean of menacing, featureless sand.

   Their sheer exhaustion was like a weight they were forced to carry on their shoulders. They walked, stumbled, kept on walking, their **misery deepening**. They were so weak that after the rest stops they could hardly rise to their feet and take up the struggle again.

2. There was not a bit of shelter to be found. No rock or tree, nothing but an unending glare. It was like walking through the cinders of a barbecue. He knew his epic struggle was coming to an end. He was tantalisingly close but his body was weakening with every step.

   Finally, unable to walk another step, he slumped on the floor and **lay corpse-like**, **his head swimming**, his skin scorched.

SECTION 1 – SETTING

WORDS

Nouns	**Sand**, dunes
	Wind, breeze, storm, ripples, waves
	Shelter, rock, tree, bushes
	Glare, air, heat, furnace
	Night, day

Similes/ Metaphors	**Sea**, ocean, wall, slow snakes, furnace, cinders, phantoms, hyena
Adjectives	**Flat**, rocky, thorny, bare, stark, barren
	Endless, sprawling
	Burning, roasting, scorching, shimmering
	Savage, merciless, vicious, menacing, agonising, tortuous
	Huge, great, mile-high
	Whining, moaning
Verbs	**Spread**, stretched
	Rose, crept, settled
	Burnt, baked, beat, suffocated
	Blew, flung, threw, whipped, chased, shifted, rolled, swirled, billowed
	Shimmered, blinded, dazzled, shrouded

PHRASES – NOUNS AND ADJECTIVES

* A land where each kilometre . . .
* For ever changing
* Impossible to find the way back
* Impossible to tell the difference between . . .
* *Great sprawling desert*
* Sea of sand
* Miles of desert, ominous and deadly
* Endless, flat horizon
* Great ocean of menacing, featureless sand
* *Huge sand dunes*
* Mile-high walls of sand
* Desert storm of sand walls
* Slow snakes of sand
* *Stark and barren*
* Rocky and spiked with thorny bushes
* *Land of burning sand*
* Not a bit of shelter
* No rock or tree, nothing but an unending glare
* Heat waves
* Ripples of heat
* Burning, merciless furnace of glare and death
* Roasting air like a blast from an open furnace

- During the hottest part of the day . . .
- More vicious than ever
- Agonising cold of the night, as torturous as the daytime heat
- *Light breeze*
- Wind against her face
- Swirling sand
- *Pitch black*
- In the glimmer of the flashlight
- Like phantoms coming to life in the evening's fading light
- *Hyena whine of the cold desert wind*
- Moaning rush of the wind
- Ugly stench of decay
- *His only companion*

PHRASES – VERBS

- Appeared and then vanished in front of them
- Spread out before him
- Stretched as far as the eye could see
- Looked exactly like the last
- *Shimmered in the heat*
- Baked by day and chilled by night
- Dazzled by the glare of the fiery sun
- Burst into the sky
- Signalled another day of hideous torture
- Shimmered and danced on the sand
- Settled like an oppressive blanket
- Like walking through cinders
- Beat down like a blacksmith's hammer against red hot iron
- Suffocating as it reflected off the sun-baked surface
- *Stirred up the sand*
- Rose from the ground
- Chased along the ground
- Rolled sideways like a wave
- Threw up clouds of dust
- Whipped up mile-high walls of sand
- Shifted relentlessly like ghostly armies
- Became rough with the airborne sand
- Brought with it . . .
- Whipped up into a fury
- Flung the sand into their throats and eyes
- Became more powerful with every step they took
- Blown away by the sandstorm and dumped elsewhere
- *Swirled into his nose and ears*

- ✷ Whipped into any exposed flesh
- ✷ Blinded them
- ✷ *Added to the cover of darkness*
- ✷ Shrouded all visibility
- ✷ Nothing moved except the shadows
- ✷ Crept and lengthened behind the rocks
- ✷ Played weird tricks on the eyes
- ✷ Faded in the distance
- ✷ Left the desert dead and silent once again
- ✷ Howled, billowed and swirled around every corner
- ✷ Hissed with insects

SENTENCES

Ahead lay miles of desert, ominous and deadly.

It was a land where each kilometre looked exactly like the last.

The desert spread out before him – a sea of sand, shimmering with heat, rocky and spiked with thorny bushes and hissing with insects.

The desert was a burning, merciless furnace of glare and death, and bleached skeletons of dead men who had been lost in the great ocean of menacing, featureless sand.

It was a land of burning sands, scarred by the wind, baked by day and chilled at night.

The agonising cold of the night was as torturous as the daytime heat.

Already the sun was bursting into the sky and signalling another day of hideous torture.

There was not a bit of shelter to be found. No rock or tree, nothing but an unending glare.

Heat waves shimmered and danced on the sand, settling like an oppressive blanket on the great sprawling desert.

The light breeze brought with it roasting air like a blast from an open furnace and an ugly stench of decay, which became more powerful with every step they took.

They felt as if they were walking through the cinders of a barbecue.

During the hottest part of the day, the sun beat down like a blacksmith's hammer against red hot iron.

They were dazzled by the glare of the fiery sun. The heat was suffocating as it reflected off the sun-baked surface.

The wind stirred up the sand, which swirled into his nose and ears.

As the breeze rose, slow snakes of sand rose from the ground, throwing up clouds of dust, and the wind against her face suddenly became rough with the airborne sand.

The sandstorm whipped up mile-high walls of sand and shrouded all visibility. As it swirled, it flung the sand into their throats and eyes.

The sea of sand dunes shifted relentlessly like ghostly armies.

In front of him, the dunes shifted, rolling sideways like a wave.

It was impossible to find the way back. The desert landscape was forever changing as huge, sand dunes disappeared, blown away by the sand storms and dumped elsewhere.

The wind had risen and the sand was more vicious than ever, chasing along the ground, whipping into any exposed flesh, blinding them.

It was pitch black and the swirling sand added to the cover of darkness.

Not a breath of air stirred. Nothing moved except the shadows that crept and lengthened behind the rocks like phantoms coming to life in the evening's fading light.

In the glimmer of the flashlight, shadows formed and played weird tricks on the eyes.

The hyena whine of the cold desert wind was his only companion.

The only sound that came was the moaning rush of the wind.

The sound faded in the distance, leaving the desert dead and silent once again.

The sand howled, billowed and swirled around every corner until it was impossible to tell the difference between the walls that appeared and then vanished in front of them and those that were meant to be there.

SECTION 2 – INTERACTION

WORDS	
Nouns	**Head**, brow, chin, mouth, breath, nose, eyes, sockets
	Chest, shoulders, stomach, middle, hips, arms, hands, fists, legs, knees, feet
Adjectives	**Heavy**, stiff, tired, weary, exhausted, dizzy, corpse-like
	Painful, wild, savage, searing, cramping
	Half-mad, spread-eagled

Verbs	**Fell**, sank, bowed, sagged
	Opened, closed, pinched
	Pressed, tugged, buried, wrapped, grabbed, twisted, clenched, clutched
	Gasped, panted, shivered, shuddered, thrashed
	Bent, curled, hunched, slouched, slumped, buckled, huddled, lay, lolled, sprawled
	Limped, hobbled, dragged, struggled, writhed
Adverbs	**Shakily**, unsteadily
	Tightly, fiercely, violently

PHRASES – NOUNS AND ADJECTIVES

* Epic struggle
* Tantalisingly close
* *Scarcely doing more than a mile in an hour*
* Painfully slow progress, little more than a shuffle
* Bodies weakening with every step
* Dreadfully weak and wasted
* Little strength left in his legs
* Sheer exhaustion was like a weight on their shoulders
* Legs as heavy as if a ball and chain had been attached to them
* Like a fish that had been reeled in and dumped onto the sand
* Like one of the walking wounded from a battlefield
* Twisted knee
* With one final gasp . . . .

PHRASES – VERBS

* Stood with hands on hips
* Hunched her shoulders
* Slumped into his chest
* *Kicked the sand and dust into the air*
* Filled their eyes, their noses, their ears, their mouths
* *Flicked his tongue round his lips*
* Tried to get some moisture to his mouth and lips
* *Could barely walk*
* Could barely put one foot in front of the other
* Made slow progress
* Forced himself forward

* Kept on moving
* Forged on until they reached . . .
* Plodded on, heads down, silent
* Trudged slowly and painfully along
* Could only shuffle along
* Dragged his feet across the ground
* Wasn't really walking, just falling forward
* Walked, stumbled, kept on walking
* Limped slowly, his foot dragging behind him, scraping on the sand
* Hobbled over the dune
* *Struggled into a sitting position*
* Got unsteadily to his feet
* Rose shakily and managed to stagger to his feet
* Got harder and harder to get to her feet
* Tried to get up, his hands behind him, his legs bent sideways
* Crumpled under his weight . . . couldn't move
* Attempted to stand, but the effort was too great
* *Wrapped her arm around him*
* Tried to support him and urge him on
* Leaned heavily on . . .
* Clutched his T-shirt
* *Unable to walk another step*
* Had nothing left
* Staggered to a halt
* Sagged limply
* Fell back against the wall
* Fell in a struggling heap
* Buckled under her
* Sank to the ground
* Fell to his knees . . . defeated
* Sprawled on the sand
* Slumped to his hands and knees in the sand
* Rolled limply onto the ground
* Curled into a ball
* Huddled in a heap
* Lay spread-eagled
* Lay corpse-like

SENTENCES

They plodded on, heads down, silent.

They covered their faces with their makeshift turbans, leaving only tiny slits for their eyes. Peering down, they could only see the ground a few metres in front of them.

Unable to walk another step, she slumped on the floor and lay corpse-like, her head swimming with tiredness.

His legs buckled under him and he slumped on the sand, legs splayed and his eyes rolling back in their sockets.

He tried to get up, his hands behind him, his legs bent sideways, but his arms crumpled under his weight. He couldn't move.

He was so tired he could barely walk, but he kept on moving, dragging his feet across the ground, shoulders stooped and his head slumped on his chest.

Holding his breath and gritting his teeth, he rose shakily and managed to stagger to his feet.

He limped slowly away, with his foot dragging behind him and scraping on the sand.

Staggering to a halt, she slumped to the ground.

Except for short rest stops, they had to forge on until they reached the track.

They walked on for hours. Dreadfully weak and wasted, their progress was slow and gradually became no more than a plodding stumble.

Their sheer exhaustion was like a weight they were forced to carry on their shoulders.

They walked, stumbled, kept on walking, their misery deepening. They were so weak that after the rest stops they could hardly rise to their feet and take up the struggle again.

They made painfully slow progress, little more than a shuffle that kicked the sand and dust into the air and filled their eyes, their noses, their ears, their mouths.

Unable to walk another step, he slumped on the floor and lay corpse-like, his head swimming, his skin scorched.

His twisted knee meant that he could only shuffle along like one of the walking wounded from a battlefield.

He fell to his knees . . . defeated. He attempted to stand, but the effort was too great and he slumped to his hands and knees in the sand. His body was wasting away. He had nothing left.

His throat was parched and his breath was coming in painful gasps. Swallowing hard, he flicked his tongue round his lips and tried to draw some moisture to his mouth and lips.

He was badly dehydrated and the sweat on his body had crusted into a fine layer of white salt crystals. Slowly, he trickled water past his swollen tongue and drained the last drops of water from the canister.

She scraped out a burrow in the sand and crawled into it. Then she huddled in a ball, shivering and sleeping fitfully until dawn.

Burrowing in the sand, they covered their bodies during the heat of the day, and shielded themselves from the blazing sun. The gentle pressure of the sand gave some relief to their tired muscles.

He had little strength left in his legs. He faltered and almost fell. Wrapping her arm around him, clutching his T-shirt, she tried desperately to support him and urge him on. Leaning heavily on Kitty, he forced himself forward.

She hooked a hand in his belt so that they wouldn't lose each other in a sudden, blinding wall of sand.

SECTION 3 – REACTION

WORDS	

Nouns	**Willpower**, determination
	Sleep, tiredness, exhaustion, fatigue
	Head, chest, face, chin, nose, nostrils, throat, mouth, lip, tongue, teeth, saliva, breath
	Eyes, sockets, eyelids, whites, tears
	Stomach, muscles, arms, fist, legs, feet, step
	Pain, agony, grimace, spasm, anguish
	Grip, grasp, vice, poison, acid, bile
	Cramps, ache
	Sores, blisters, scabs
	Sigh, whimper, whine, groan, moan, gasp, cry, scream, yell, shriek, howl, wail
Similes/ Metaphors	**Lead weights**, pieces of wood, jackhammer
Adjectives	**Heavy**, stiff, tired, weary, exhausted, dizzy, faint, light-headed, breathless, corpse-like
	White, pale, grey, pink, red, bloodshot
	Wide, gaping, bulging, deathly, lifeless
	Dull, heavy, drooping, sagging, heavy-lidded
	Burning, razor-edged, claw-like, overwhelming
	Wild, fierce, stinging, searing, hammering

Small, low, wild, ragged, deathly, painful, piercing, high-pitched, ear-splitting

Verbs   **Closed**, shut, drooped, fluttered, rolled, bulged, squeezed, scrunched

Burnt, twisted, jerked, gripped, grasped, churned, gnawed, tightened, contracted

Bit, gritted, rubbed

Staggered, rocked, buckled, crashed

Throbbed, ached, stung, pounded, hammered

Gasped, gulped, whispered, sighed, whined, groaned, moaned, muttered, mumbled, murmured, croaked, faltered, whimpered, cried, yelled, howled, wailed

Let out, uttered, released

Adverbs   **Weakly**, feebly, painfully

PHRASES – NOUNS AND ADJECTIVES

* Endless struggle
* Monumental task of sheer willpower and determination
* Gaunt, his body parched and wasted
* *Dark, deep lines of pain*
* Grey shadows under deep, sunken eyes and cheeks
* Face deathly white and eyes lifeless
* *Light-headed with exhaustion and dehydration*
* Legs heavy like pieces of wood
* Every step was an effort
* *Sagging, lifeless, red-rimmed eyes*
* Blood-shot eyes
* Only the whites of her eyes were visible
* Like needles sticking in her eyes
* Glare of the sun had done its damage
* Every time he opened his eyes . . .
* *Like a vice around his chest*
* Pain was overwhelming
* Every second the pain . . .
* Like an acid burning his stomach
* As if a poison had taken root in his gut
* Hammering pain in his head
* Fierce grimace

* *Small whimper*
* Low, painful wheeze
* Low, gurgling groan
* Deathly moan
* With one final gasp . . .
* Painful gasps
* High-pitched howl
* Ear-splitting yell
* Wild, ragged wail
* *Flaking skin*
* Sores around his lips
* Swollen, red blisters
* Tired and blistered feet
* Mass of angry sores and peeling skin
* Cracked, swollen, scorched lips
* Through cracked and bleeding lips
* Small lacerations on his lips and cheeks
* *Cracked ankle*
* Twisted knee

PHRASES – VERBS

* Couldn't carry on much longer
* Dragged down by an irresistible urge to sleep
* Made him light-headed
* Etched on his gaunt face
* *Seeped into her eyes*
* Encrusted with sand
* Reddened by fatigue and lack of water
* Screwed their eyes up
* Rolled in her head
* Dared not open his eyes
* Burnt into his eyes and brain
* Felt as if the pain in his head might explode through his skull
* Covered them with the cloth of their makeshift turbans
* Peered down through the tiny slits
* Saw only the ground a few metres in front of them
* *Gripped his head like a clenched fist*
* Beat like a jackhammer
* Hunched her shoulders against the pain
* Sent a shock wave of pain through his . . .
* Coursed up and down his legs
* Stabbed into his hips

- ☀ Gnawed at his feet
- ☀ Twisted in agony as he . . .
- ☀ *Tore through her stomach*
- ☀ Could feel the bile rising at the back of her throat
- ☀ Retched violently, her mouth gaping like a fish out of water
- ☀ *Swollen inside his boot*
- ☀ Took off his boot and peeled off his sock
- ☀ *Running a fever*
- ☀ Burning and sweat pouring off her
- ☀ Starting to become delirious
- ☀ Twisted his head from side to side
- ☀ Muttered, rambling unintelligible words
- ☀ Cried out at some dreadful image
- ☀ *Fluttered open briefly*
- ☀ *Mumbled weakly*
- ☀ Whined that he couldn't go any further
- ☀ Let out a small whimper
- ☀ Slurred with fatigue and overexposure to the heat
- ☀ *Melting like a wax candle*
- ☀ Hammered his brain to a pulp
- ☀ Moistened their lips from their scanty supply of water
- ☀ Sucked on pebbles
- ☀ Dreamt that he was bathing in a running stream
- ☀ Woke to find himself in a sea of sand
- ☀ *Coated his body like powdered sugar*
- ☀ Felt like an old piece of leather
- ☀ Dried and cracked in the intense heat of the desert
- ☀ Whipped against his skin
- ☀ Pressed his lips together to stop it entering his mouth
- ☀ Bowed his head into his shoulder so that he could breathe
- ☀ Squeezed as if a boa constrictor had coiled around his chest
- ☀ Squeezed his wheezing breath from him

SENTENCES

His face was gaunt, his body parched and wasted.

Dark, deep lines of pain were etched on his gaunt face; grey shadows under deep, sunken eyes and cheeks.

Exhaustion and dehydration had made him light-headed. He lay on the floor, dragged down by an irresistible urge to sleep.

Just rising to their feet was a monumental task of sheer willpower and determination.

His eyes were bloodshot and rimmed with red. His vision was blurred.

Fine sand had seeped into her eyes. It was as if they had needles sticking in them.

Her face was deathly white, encrusted with sand, and her sagging eyes were lifeless. The endless struggle had drained them of all expression.

Her sunken eyes were reddened by fatigue and lack of water.

His bloodshot eyes were almost closed from fatigue, lungs sucking in the hot air with painful gasps, heart beating like a jackhammer.

Every nerve in his body screamed at him as the pain gripped his head like a clenched fist.

His face was a mass of sores and peeling skin.

His face reddened and twisted in agony as he took off his boot and peeled off his sock.

Every movement sent a shock wave of pain through his tired and blistered feet.

The pain coursed up and down his legs, stabbing into his hips, and gnawing at his feet.

He dared not open his eyes, the glare of the sun had done its damage, burning into his eyes and brain. Every time he opened his eyes it felt as if the pain in his head might explode through his skull.

Every second the pain was getting worse. He couldn't carry on much longer. His cracked ankle had swollen inside his boot and he couldn't put any weight on it.

She was running a fever, her skin burning and sweat pouring off her.

He was starting to become delirious, twisting his head from side to side, muttering, rambling unintelligible words, crying out at some dreadful image.

Her eyes fluttered open and she mumbled weakly through cracked and bleeding lips.

He kept stopping every few metres, whining that he couldn't go any further.

He slumped with his hands on his knees, gasping for breath – and when he eventually spoke his voice was a low, painful wheeze.

His voice slurred with fatigue and overexposure to the heat.

He felt as if he was melting like a wax candle.

The searing heat and glare from the relentless sun hammered his brain to a pulp.

They lay panting and every now and again moistening their lips from their scanty supply of water.

He had been dreaming that he was bathing in a running stream, with green banks, but woke to find himself in an arid wilderness.

A fine layer of sand coated his body like powdered sugar.

Her lips and eyelids were stuck together.

She felt like an old piece of leather, drying and cracking in the intense heat of the desert.

The stinging sand whipped against his skin, and he had to press his lips together to stop it entering his mouth. He bowed his head into his shoulder so that he could breathe.

His lungs became tight and constricted as if a boa constrictor had coiled around his chest and was squeezing his wheezing breath from him.

He knew their epic struggle was coming to an end. They were tantalisingly close but their bodies were weakening with every step.

16

Snow, ice and avalanches

THE S/C-I-R STRUCTURE

There was a muffled rumble and, without warning, the snow burst through the trees, barrelling down the mountain. **In that one instant, she felt a chill, steely fist squeeze her heart and freeze her to the spot.**

The slide moved in surges, like a rollercoaster, crashed through the trees, snapping their limbs and shredding bark from their trunks – and accelerated as the slope steepened, adding debris to its menacing load. As it rushed towards her, **blind instinct took over from sheer panic as she desperately tried to remember the safety drill.**

When the snow hit, she struck out vigorously with her arms, swimming as hard as she could for the surface, trying to keep her head up to the surface and holding her breath so that she didn't get bunged up with snow.

SECTION 1 – SETTING

WORDS

Nouns	**Horizon**, ocean, sea, wave, clouds, plumes, blast, dust
	Iceberg, ice, icicles, ice-spicules, frost
	Crystals, flakes, daggers, sculptures, cocoons
	Boulders, rocks
	Avalanche, slide, air blast, hurricane, tornado

Village, town, street, alley, buildings, house, roof, windows, trees

Stillness, silence, hiss, whisper, rumble, crack, snap, splinter, shudder, buzz, roar, shriek

Snowmobiles, ice-probes, skis, sticks

Motion, reaction, succession

Similes/ Metaphors

Desert of ice, pillowing quilt, puff of smoke, vaporous tentacles, ghostly fingers, fine flour, white tidal wave, boiling wave, runaway train, concrete, plaster of Paris cast

Adjectives

Thick, white, snow-draped

Bleak, bitter, cold, icy, frozen

Whirling, billowy, wind-whipped, shuffling, rolling

Needle-pointed, dangerous, lethal, explosive

Lightning-quick, thunderous

Great, massive, miniature

Distant, low, growling, whistling, drumming, howling, roaring

Verbs

Fell, lay, heaped, surrounded, buried, blanketed, floated

Crunched, cracked, vibrated, trembled, quivered, rocked, pounded

Split, shattered, slid, spilled, barrelled, surged, burst, jetted, plunged, lurched, hurtled, careered

Lifted, thrown, propelled, peeled, tore, blasted, whipped, toppled, rolled

Grew, accelerated

PHRASES – NOUNS AND ADJECTIVES

- From somewhere above them
- *Silently, softly like a thief*
- Like fine flour clouding through a sieve
- Vaporous tentacles like ghostly fingers
- *Billowy, white ocean*
- White wall of flakes
- Shawl of snow
- Thick, white pillowing quilt of snow
- Wind-whipped snow

* Nothing but snow-draped trees for miles in either direction
* In piles on the dark road
* No horizon to the white world
* *Chain reaction*
* In lightning-quick succession
* *A bitter whirl of icy crystals*
* Trees like ice sculptures
* Frozen cocoons of long icicles
* Bleak desert of ice and nothing but silence
* Driving wall of needle-pointed ice-spicules
* Vast iceberg
* Frozen, cascade of water
* Near-lethal in its ferocity
* *Thick, muffled silence*
* Not a whisper of sound
* Silence, an eerie, unsettling silence, stillness
* Muffled rumble
* Hiss of skis
* Snapping, splintering sound
* Shivery rattle
* Audible crack in the snow below her skis
* Distant rumble like thunder
* Low, growling sound
* Whoosh of sound
* Howling jet-stream of snow overhead
* Sudden explosive crack of ice
* Shudder of cracking ice
* Shuffling, roaring slide
* Thunderous drumming noise
* Like a runaway train shrieking towards her
* Great whistling hurricane
* Chainsaw buzz of snowmobiles
* *Growing, powder cloud, a white mist*
* Small white plume like a puff of smoke
* A faint plume of grey
* Boiling cloud of white
* *Avalanche cloud*
* Air blast
* Miniature tornadoes
* Tornado of snow and ice
* Massive wedge of snow
* Huge slab of snow
* Great spraying wall of snow
* Like a white tidal wave

- ⋆ Great, boiling wave of snow
- ⋆ Rolling snow boulders and spinning ice rocks
- ⋆ Hundreds of tons of moving snow
- ⋆ *Like concrete behind him*
- ⋆ Weight of the slide

PHRASES – VERBS

- ⋆ Began to fall in flurries
- ⋆ Froze hard again
- ⋆ Locked the land in its grip
- ⋆ Closed the roads, the tracks and paths
- ⋆ Lost in an ice-bound wilderness
- ⋆ *Seemed to happen in slow motion*
- ⋆ Had taken no more than a few terrifying powerless seconds
- ⋆ *Fell like daggers*
- ⋆ Tinkled like pieces of fallen glass
- ⋆ *Cracked and growled*
- ⋆ Split like a lightning bolt
- ⋆ Cracked in the shape of a lightning bolt
- ⋆ Turned to overlapping sheets of icicles
- ⋆ *Gushed up to gale force*
- ⋆ Felt an arctic wind blow down his spine
- ⋆ Drove before it a swirling, rushing fog of . . .
- ⋆ *Shattered and fell to the ground*
- ⋆ Sheared off, plunging, crashing into the water
- ⋆ *Swept his skis out from underneath him*
- ⋆ Rolled and tumbled its murderous way down the slope
- ⋆ Picked up speed
- ⋆ Exploded into a shower of snow boulders
- ⋆ Felt like a carpet being pulled out from underneath him
- ⋆ Burst through the trees with no warning
- ⋆ Shattered and spilled down the slope
- ⋆ Barrelled down the mountains
- ⋆ Crashed through the trees, snapped their limbs and shredded bark from their trunks
- ⋆ Moved in surges, like a rollercoaster
- ⋆ Accelerated as the slope steepened
- ⋆ Propelled into the air by . . .
- ⋆ Grew larger as it moved down the slope
- ⋆ Plunged down the mountainside towards . . .
- ⋆ Rose like thunderheads
- ⋆ Could destroy a building as effectively as a bomb
- ⋆ *Creaked to a halt and silence*

* Flickered out . . . plunged into darkness
* *Felt a strange vibration through the soles of his feet*
* Trembled beneath his feet
* Quivered on its foundations
* Rocked violently
* Whipped down the street
* Hurtled past the door
* Blasted over the roof, pummelling down and streaming into the town
* Lifted off its foundations
* Peeled off the roof like playing cards
* Floated in the air towards him
* Lurched and the windows smashed inwards
* Thrown through the glass windows like a monstrous projectile
* Tore through the wall, wrenched free the window frames
* Jetted into the room through the broken panes
* *Pounded the side of the car*
* Careered along on two wheels
* Toppled it over on its side
* Began to roll over faster and faster

SENTENCES

They were lost in an ice-bound wilderness; surrounded by ice, which cracked and growled under their weight, and occasionally split like a lightning bolt.

A bleak desert of ice and nothing but silence. Not a sound, not a whisper of sound came out of the desolation.

They clung to one another, struggling to see in the wind-whipped snow, which stung their faces.

They were caught in an ice-storm that rose and swirled and subsided with the icy wind that gushed up to gale force, driving a wall of swirling, rushing needle-pointed ice-spicules capable of shattering glass.

He could hear an almost constant grinding, crashing and deep-throated booming as millions of tons of ice twisted, screeched and roared, tore and cracked.

The ice shattered and fell to the ground, tinkling like pieces of fallen glass.

There was a sudden explosive crack of ice. A vast iceberg sheared off and crashed into the water beside the boat.

Outside, the snow froze hard again and locked the land in its grip, closed the roads, the tracks and paths.

They found the base of a waterfall, but it had frozen, cascading water turned to overlapping, rippling sheets of icicles.

A small white plume arose like a puff of smoke and a huge slab of snow slid away from the mountain, like a dinner plate sliding off a table. A shuffling, roaring slide, rolling and tumbling its murderous way down the slope.

There was a muffled rumble and, without warning, the snow burst through the trees, barrelling down the mountain.

The distant rumble like thunder grew louder and the ground beneath his feet seemed to shiver and shake. It was accompanied by a snapping, splintering sound and a rising howl of wind.

It was a chain reaction, one event followed another in lightning-quick succession.

It moved in surges, like a rollercoaster, crashed through the trees, snapping their limbs and shredding bark from their trunks – and accelerated as the slope steepened, adding debris to its menacing load.

There was a growing, boiling powder cloud, a white mist propelled into the air by hundreds of tons of moving snow plunging down the mountainside.

The whole of the upper slope was boiling and seething, clouds of snow rising like thunderheads, miniature tornadoes forming along its edges, and pouring down the mountainside.

An air blast began to develop in front of the rapidly moving snow, a travelling shock wave which could destroy a building as effectively as a bomb.

He felt a strange vibration through the soles of his feet.

From the end of the street came a sudden and sustained gust of wind that whipped down the street, and a tornado of snow and ice hurtled past the door.

It seemed to happen in slow motion, but it had taken no more than a few terrifying powerless seconds.

A great wall of snow blasted over the roof, pummelling down and streaming into the town like a white tidal wave.

The garage lifted off its foundations and floated in the air towards him.

The air quivered and the noise grew a little louder. She did not hear the end of the sentence because the noise reached a deafening pitch. A thunderous drumming noise overhead. Then the avalanche hit.

The house quivered on its foundations, lurched and then the windows smashed inwards.

Fine snow dust jetted into the room through the broken panes as though squirted from a great hosepipe.

The air blast slammed at the large van parked outside, rocked it violently, toppled it over on its side. Pushed by the snow, it began to roll faster and faster and then was swept up and hurled through the window like a monstrous projectile.

A howling jet-stream of snow that sounded like a runaway train shrieking towards her tore through the walls, snatched the window frames and hurled them after the glass.

It creaked to a halt and everything went quiet as though the whole town was holding its breath.

SECTION 2 – INTERACTION

WORDS

Nouns	**Head**, mask, chest, arms, legs
	Hope, strength
	Weight
Similes/ Metaphors	**Raft of ice**, sheet of ice, snow surfboard, pinball machine, icy womb, windscreen wiper
Adjectives	**Vicious**, driving, crushing
	Pitch-black
	Icy, frozen
Verbs	**Clambered**, shuffled, scrabbled, scrambled, swam
	Slipped, slid, stumbled, tumbled, fell, plummeted
	Dug, gripped, rammed, jammed, grabbed, lunged, hauled, levered
	Balanced, dangled, swung
	Sucked, swept, flung, dragged
	Struck, slammed, bombarded, ripped, pinned, held fast, locked, crushed, compressed, submerged
	Wiggled, wriggled, flicked, pushed, clawed
	Spat, expanded, inhaled, exhaled, suffocated
	Dropped, exploded
	Felt, found

PHRASES – NOUNS AND ADJECTIVES

* It was then, without warning, that . . .
* Within seconds . . .
* With her last ounce of strength
* *Frozen fingers*
* Gloved hand
* Slightest slip of her fingers
* Vicious jerk of the rope
* *Crack underneath her*
* Slab she was standing on
* Snow surfboard
* Like being in a pinball machine
* Behind him, around him, over him
* Everything the avalanche had carried, including Kitty
* *Ice mask*
* Crushing weight of snow on her chest
* In her pitch-black icy womb
* *Just enough space for her to . . .*
* Sizeable amount of space in front of her
* Without the small pocket of air for her mouth and nose
* *Both arms were free*
* Legs directly above him
* Top of his head against the snow

PHRASES – VERBS

* When the snow hit . . .
* When she felt herself slowing down . . .
* Just as he was giving up hope . . .
* *Clambered over, slipped, slid and fell across the ice*
* Slipping and scrambling on all fours
* Groped with his arms and found thin air
* Sent tumbling into the void
* Halted his fall
* *Found a fist-sized hole*
* Lunged with her right hand
* Scrabbled with her fingers for a grip
* Took the full weight of her body
* Rammed her left arm into the crack in the ice
* Dug in with her boots
* Jammed the front spikes of her crampons
* Couldn't find a grip

- ⭑ Brought her leg up
- ⭑ Swung out from the crack
- ⭑ Swung perilously over the drop
- ⭑ Hauled herself up
- ⭑ Levered herself upwards
- ⭑ Balanced precariously
- ⭑ Began to slip
- ⭑ Dangled over the sheer drop
- ⭑ Would send her plummeting down
- ⭑ Made it to the top
- ⭑ *Stumbled on, shuffling blindly on all fours*
- ⭑ Bombarded by the blast of driving hail
- ⭑ Threatened to blow them off their feet
- ⭑ Gripped whatever they could get hold of
- ⭑ Stopped themselves being flung from their feet
- ⭑ *Stood there, frozen to the spot*
- ⭑ Searched for a way out
- ⭑ Wiggled the skis with only a slight pressure from her toes
- ⭑ Stopped, and tried it again
- ⭑ Tried to edge away from the slab
- ⭑ *Sucked under like a surfer caught in a deadly wave*
- ⭑ Swept downhill by the hurtling torrent of snow
- ⭑ Dragged head-over-heels, rotating violently towards the trees
- ⭑ Tumbled uncontrollably inside the current of raging snow
- ⭑ Gathered momentum
- ⭑ *Struck out vigorously with her arms*
- ⭑ Swam as hard as she could for the surface
- ⭑ Tried to keep her head up to the surface
- ⭑ Held her breath so that she didn't get bunged up with snow
- ⭑ *Slammed her into trees*
- ⭑ Ripped her away to continue her ominous descent
- ⭑ Pinned him to the tree
- ⭑ Submerged in a white blanket – an icy cocoon
- ⭑ *Brought her left arm across her face*
- ⭑ Kept his hands raised over his head to preserve a pocket of air
- ⭑ Saved his right arm from being crushed between him and the tree
- ⭑ Give her air space to breathe
- ⭑ Enabled her to dig a hole around her face
- ⭑ *Spat out the snow to keep her airway clear*
- ⭑ Expanded his chest by filling his lungs with air
- ⭑ Would have created a suffocating ice mask
- ⭑ Formed over his face each time his breath froze to his face
- ⭑ *Frozen into an icy cocoon the moment the slide stopped*
- ⭑ Could not move her legs

* Held fast in what felt like a plaster of Paris cast
* Couldn't lift her head
* Locked into the ice in a concrete pillow
* *Flicked the snow from her mouth*
* Used her left hand like a windscreen wiper
* Pushed with her arms
* Scrabbled at the snow
* Wriggled her elbow and wrist
* Clawed at the snow around her head and shoulders
* Compressed the snow to make an even bigger space
* *Felt the grip on her right arm ease gradually*
* Slid onto her face and dropped into her collar
* Exploded down onto her shoulder
* *Gathered spit onto his lip*
* Used his tongue to push the saliva from his mouth
* Slid down his nose . . . lying on his back
* *Heard a noise above him*
* Grabbed him underneath the arms
* Hauled him out

SENTENCES

They clambered over, slipped, slid and fell across the ice.

Slipping and scrambling on all fours across the cracked, rising raft of ice, he groped with his arms and found thin air. He was sent tumbling into the void until a vicious jerk of the rope halted his fall.

She hauled herself up, finding a fist-sized hole in which she could jam the front spikes of her crampons. She brought her leg up, balancing precariously, then jammed her left arm into the crack in the ice which ran up the corner of the cliff.

Here the ice was a featureless, smooth sheet; she knew the spikes of her crampons would find no grip on the face, that her feet would be dangling over the sheer drop, and that the slightest slip of her fingers would send her plummeting down.

She lunged with her right hand, and took the full weight of her body as she swung out from the crack.

Her heart raced as she felt her gloved hand beginning to slip; her frozen fingers scrabbling as her body swung perilously over the drop.

Desperately, she scrabbled with her fingers for a grip. She dug in with her boots and levered herself upwards, and with her last ounce of strength, she had made it to the top.

The air around them was filled with dagger-like pieces of ice. They stumbled on, shuffling blindly on all fours, bombarded by the blast of driving hail, which threatened to blow them off their feet. They gripped whatever they could get hold of to stop themselves being flung from their feet.

It was then, without warning, that the slope she was standing on started to move like a carpet sliding across a polished floor.

There was a crack underneath her and the slab she was standing on split into two sections.

She stood there, frozen to the spot, searching for a way out. Cracks had appeared all around her. She was on a snow surfboard that could be set off at any second.

Holding her breath, she wiggled the skis with only a slight pressure from her toes, stopped, and tried it again, desperately trying to edge away from the slab.

Within seconds, she was sucked under like a surfer caught in a deadly wave. She was swept downhill by the hurtling torrent of snow, tumbling uncontrollably, pulled head-over-heels, rotating violently towards the trees.

When the snow hit, she struck out vigorously with her arms, swimming as hard as she could for the surface, trying to keep her head up to the surface and holding her breath so that she didn't get bunged up with snow.

It was like being in a pinball machine, as she tumbled uncontrollably inside the current of raging snow which gathered momentum, slammed her into trees, and then ripped her away to continue her ominous descent.

As he was slammed into the tree, the rest of the snow swept in behind him, around him, over him, pinning him to the tree, completely submerging him in a white blanket – an icy cocoon.

He kept his hands raised over his head to preserve a pocket of air, which saved his right arm from being crushed between him and the tree.

When she felt herself slowing down, she brought her left arm across her face, but not too close, to give her air space to breathe and enable her to dig a hole around her face.

Everything the avalanche had carried, including Kitty, was frozen into an icy cocoon the moment the slide stopped.

She could not move her legs which were held fast in what felt like a plaster of Paris cast, nor lift her head, which was locked into the ice in a concrete pillow. She spat out the snow to keep her airway clear.

He expanded his chest by filling his lungs with air so that he would have more room to breathe when the snow had settled. Without this, his first breaths would have created a suffocating ice mask.

There was a crushing weight of snow on her chest.

In this pitch-black icy womb, there was just enough space for her to use her left hand like a windscreen wiper to flick the snow from her mouth.

She clawed at the snow around her head and shoulders and felt the grip on her right arm ease gradually. She wriggled her elbow and wrist. First, a shower of icy flakes slid onto her face and dropped into her collar and then a large lump of icy snow exploded down onto her shoulder.

Now she had both arms free and a sizeable amount of space in front of her, she was able to push with her arms and compress the snow to make an even bigger space.

He gathered spit onto his lip and used his tongue to push it from his mouth. As it slid down his nose, he realised he was lying on his back with his legs directly above him, the top of his head pressed against the snow.

Just as he was giving up hope, he heard a noise above him and hands scrabbling at the snow. A hand grabbed him underneath the arms and hauled him out.

He was halfway across the street when he stopped in his tracks. He felt the ground begin to tremble underfoot, turned and saw the approaching snow cloud grow larger, higher and plunging towards the town.

He ran down the street, an icy dread coursing through his blood. He was knocked off his feet, sent sprawling to the road in a spinning heap as a great plume of snow buried him up to his chest.

Desperately, he hauled himself out of the snow, fell against the wall, and tried to scuffle back along the street.

SECTION 3 – REACTION

WORDS	
Nouns	**Instant**, moment, time, position
	Instinct, dread, panic, calm
	Sleep, surrender, fight
	Stomach, back, spine, forehead, mouth, chest, heart, pulse, oxygen
	Pain, agony, blood, trickle, goose-bumps
	Whimper, roar
Similes/ Metaphors	**Like a vice**, shivering wave of terror, an agony of daggers
Adjectives	**Sheer**, blind, desperate, urgent
	Jagged, searing, tremendous, excruciating

Rasping, painful, pitiful

Cold, icy, steely

Verbs   **Felt**, knew, tried, fought, rejected, repressed

Jolted, kick-started

Squeezed, tightened, twisted, spread, subsided

Dripped

PHRASES – NOUNS AND ADJECTIVES

★ In that one instant . . .
★ But the next moment . . .
★ A single word – avalanche
★ *No time to think, no time to do anything*
★ Blind instinct took over from sheer panic
★ *Cold, icy dread*
★ As cold as the ice tomb that encased her
★ *Something in the desperate urgency of the shout*
★ Even though his heart was pounding . . .
★ *Frozen snow inside his nostrils*
★ Trickle of warm blood
★ Jagged, lightning slice of searing pain

PHRASES – VERBS

★ Knew then what it was
★ Knew he had only seconds before it arrived
★ Had to get out of there and fast
★ Tried to remember the safety drill
★ Knew he had ended up in the worst possible position
★ Fought a wave of desperation . . .
★ Tried to think what to do
★ Knew if she was to live she had to . . .
★ Reject sleep, reject surrender and fight for her life
★ Knew he had to remain calm
★ Repress the rising tide of panic
★ *Jolted him out of his paralysis*
★ Kick-started his survival instincts
★ Had to move. Do something
★ *Felt icy fingers close round her heart*
★ Felt a chill, steely fist squeeze her heart

- ☆ Spread into his chest
- ☆ Squeezed like a vice
- ☆ Sent a shivering wave of terror down his spine
- ☆ Broke out in a shiver of goose-bumps
- ☆ *Stole into his stomach*
- ☆ Tightened and twisted
- ☆ *Came out as a rasping whisper*
- ☆ Allowed herself a pitiful whimper as she . . .
- ☆ Tried to take painful, shallow breaths
- ☆ Could not afford to burn precious oxygen
- ☆ *Froze her to the spot*
- ☆ Looked at it, mouth gaping
- ☆ *Followed by a deafening roar*
- ☆ Seemed to explode in his head
- ☆ *Felt a tremendous pain in his chest*
- ☆ Made breathing an agony of daggers in his chest
- ☆ Felt an excruciating pain in his hip
- ☆ His foot was being twisted outwards
- ☆ Shot across her back
- ☆ Dripped down his forehead, and into his mouth
- ☆ Waited until the agony subsided

SENTENCES

He knew then what it was, and knew he had only seconds before it arrived. He had to get out of there and fast.

There was no time to think, no time to do anything.

She felt icy fingers close round her heart, as cold as the ice tomb that encased her. Her stomach tightened and twisted as a single word roared in her head. It came out as a rasping whisper. Avalanche.

In that one instant, she felt a chill, steely fist squeeze her heart and freeze her to the spot. But the next moment, blind instinct took over from sheer panic as she desperately tried to remember the safety drill.

His skin broke out in a shiver of goose-bumps as the cold and the shock struck.

A cold, icy dread stole into his stomach, spread into his chest and squeezed like a vice. He knew he had ended up in the worst possible position.

Fighting a wave of desperation, she tried to think what to do. She knew if she was to live she had to reject sleep, reject surrender and fight for her life.

There was something in the desperate urgency of the shout that sent a shivering wave of terror down his spine.

A blast of freezing air slammed into him, followed by a deafening roar that seemed to explode in his head. Then he saw it and felt a tremendous pain in his chest.

He looked at it, mouth gaping, as it soared right over his house.

Even though his heart was pounding, he knew he had to remain calm and repress the rising tide of panic. He could not afford to burn precious oxygen.

The frozen snow inside his nostrils made breathing an agony of daggers in his chest.

He felt an excruciating pain in his hip; his foot was being twisted outwards.

A trickle of warm blood dripped down his forehead, and into his mouth. It jolted him out of his paralysis and kick-started his survival instincts. He had to move. Do something.

It sent a jagged, searing pain shooting across her back. Tears sprang into her eyes and she howled.

She waited until the agony subsided, allowing herself a pitiful whimper as she tried to take painful, shallow breaths.

Appendix

Planning an adventure story

1. The hero decides to go on a journey/find something special/stop a dangerous event happening

The challenge or adventure is revealed to the hero who is at home or at school with family or friends. He finds out about the new setting where the story is to take place. Describe the event that gets the hero involved in the adventure. Could it be:

The discovery of something old?

- ★ letter
- ★ newspaper article
- ★ map
- ★ diary.

The discovery of something new?

- ★ mobile phone
- ★ text
- ★ email
- ★ blog
- ★ message on Facebook
- ★ picture on Instagram
- ★ strange pop-up on the computer.

A strange, unexpected encounter?

- ★ Does it involve going on a trip?
- ★ Does it involve a challenge?

Discovery of a:

- ★ kidnap
- ★ theft

© 2016, *Descriptosaurus: Action & Adventure*, Alison Wilcox, Routledge.

* dangerous organisation
* imminent event?

2. The hero travels to the location

Describe the journey.

* Does he meet someone who may go on the journey, give advice or provide a clue that will help later?
* Does he find useful clues?

3. The adventure begins

The hero gets to the new setting, where the main adventure will take place. As he has never been there before, he needs to think about:

* what he sees, hears, smells
* whether there are any dangers/obstacles
* how the new setting makes him feel.

If there is a villain in the story, he will not appear in person, but the hero:

* will learn something about the villain
* may meet some of the villain's allies.

4. A problem occurs in the setting/The hero meets the villain's allies

Dream up scenes and events where the hero is tested:

Setting

* Plane crash in the mountains
* Stranded in the desert
* Fire in the forest

- ★ An avalanche
- ★ A boat capsizing during a storm
- ★ Flooded caves/tunnels
- ★ Lost in the jungle.

Villain

- ★ Challenged by the villain's allies – followed, pursued, escapes
- ★ Tests hero's strength, bravery and determination
- ★ Hero still does not come face-to-face with the villain
- ★ Hero will learn more about the villain, the location of the object(s), person.

Don't just tell the reader what is happening. Describe the hero's feelings and his interaction (movements/actions) with the setting and/or the villain's allies.

5. The hero is in great danger (the 'black moment')

Events take a dangerous turn. This could be as a result of:

- ★ severe weather conditions adding to the danger and chances of survival
- ★ loss of essential survival equipment, or an injury.

Describe the danger, building the atmosphere and suspense:

- ★ Describe the hero's emotions and his movements (interaction).
- ★ Ask the readers questions so that they are drawn into the battle for survival.

6. The hero comes face-to-face with the main villain

Imagine how and where the hero and villain meet:

- ★ Either the villain finds the hero, or the hero has entered one of the villain's locations and is discovered.

* Describe the route the hero takes through the setting.
* Include lots of action.
* Describe the hero's fear/nervousness.
* Build the suspense and atmosphere before they meet by including sounds and shadows.
* Ask the readers questions so that they are drawn into the story.

7. The hero survives the crisis/escapes the villain

* The hero finds somewhere to shelter or rest.
* The hero escapes from the villain.
* How does he escape?
* What new knowledge has he gained that will help him defeat the villain?

8. Climax: the final struggle/the problem is solved

Devise a plan or find something that will help him to face the ultimate danger and be rescued:

* The hero and villain meet again in the final action scene.
* Where do they meet? Describe any barriers to entering the setting.
* How does the hero defeat the villain? Did he have a plan before meeting the villain/getting to the final destination?
* Does the hero have any help?
* How is he rescued and by whom?
* How is he feeling?
* Is he injured?
* What happens to the villain?

9. Resolution

* The hero has been rescued.
* He returns home.
* How has the adventure changed the hero, e.g. does he embark on a campaign to raise funds for mountain rescue?

★ The hero has won.
★ He returns home victorious.
★ What was the result of his completing the task, e.g. did he get a reward, did he become a local hero?

Plot planning sheet

What happens to get the hero involved in the adventure?	
What does the challenge involve?	
Describe the journey and route.	
Describe the new location. *Does the hero learn anything about the villain?* *Does he meet the villain's allies?*	
What disaster happens? *How does the hero meet the villain's allies?* *Where? What happens?* *What does he learn about the villain?*	

What happens to increase the danger? *The hero meets the villain. How? Where? What happens?*	
How does the hero ease his suffering? Does he find shelter? *The hero escapes from the villain. How?*	
CLIMAX The hero is rescued. How? By whom? *The hero defeats the villain. How? Does he have help?* What happens to the villain?	
RESOLUTION The hero returns home. How has he changed?	
Additional notes	

Hero planning sheet

Name Age	
Physical description: face, eyes, voice, hairstyle, clothes Distinctive features	
What is the hero most afraid of?	
Does the hero have any secrets, skills or unusual traits?	
What are the hero's main interests?	

Who are the members of their family? What do they do? Do any of them have a secret?	
Who are their close friends? Will any of them help/hinder the hero? Do they have any special skills or secrets?	
What has the hero got to gain by achieving the task, overcoming the challenge? What has the hero got to lose if he or she fails? How does the hero change?	
Additional information	

Villain planning sheet

Name Age	
Physical description: eyes, voice, clothing, movement Distinctive features, e.g. scars	
Occupation Does the villain have any special skills, talents?	
Who are his or her allies?	
What does he or she want and why?	

Where does he or she live/ work? Describe the location. Is it very secure, scary? Are there many barriers, alarms, guards, etc.?	
Why is the hero a threat to him or her?	
What does the villain do to people who cross him or her?	
Additional information	

The race

The journey; routes; moving closer to the destination; secret passages and tunnels

SETTING/CHARACTER	INTERACTION	REACTION

The chase

Followed; hiding; pursued; trapped

SETTING/CHARACTER	INTERACTION	REACTION

Survival

Fire, explosions, earthquakes and volcanoes; in the water; deserts; snow, ice and avalanches

SETTING/CHARACTER	INTERACTION	REACTION